THE RAMBLING RECTOR

To John and Sinéad

Norman Ruddock.

*This book is dedicated to all those fellow travellers
in St Benedict's Ward, Mater Private Hospital Dublin
whose lives were cut short.
May They Rest in Peace.*

Norman Ruddock

The Rambling Rector

the columba press

First published in 2005 by
the columba press
55A Spruce Avenue, Stillorgan Industrial Park,
Blackrock, Co Dublin

Cover by Bill Bolger
Cover photo by Shay Doyle
Origination by The Columba Press
Printed in Ireland by ColourBooks Ltd, Dublin

ISBN 1 85607 511 7

Acknowledgements
My thanks to Nicholas Furlong and Patrick Semple who gave valuable
help and encouragement with this book. To Alan Ruddock who read
the manuscript and who made helpful suggestions and alterations. To
Norman, Jonathan and Catherine who typed the manuscript.

Table of Contents

Roots

On the road from Dublin, driving south, I took a detour through Rathdrum, Co Wicklow to call to the grave of my grandparents Richard and Catherine Ruddock. Like most of the other graves it was in a sorry state. The headstone was at an angle of forty-five degrees, and the grave had completely caved in. It has now been restored.

Grandfather Ruddock had been a gamekeeper on the Fitzwilliam estate at Coolattin in Co Wicklow, like his father before him. There he met my grandmother, Catherine O'Sullivan from Ballylongford in County Kerry, who worked in the big house. Catherine, born a Roman Catholic, had been fostered by a Church of Ireland family in Kerry and brought up as a Protestant. On her deathbed in Rathdrum hospital she was received back into the church of her birth by her priest-grandson Philip O'Neill.

I took my name from my uncle Norman, who spent his life as a member of the Garda Síochána in Omeath and Carlingford in Co Louth. Norman, like most of his brothers and sisters, had married a Roman Catholic, and attended Mass regularly. All my cousins on my father's side of the family were Roman Catholic. Uncle Norman retired to live in Dublin. At his funeral in Sutton, overlooking Dublin Bay, it was a strange sensation to see his coffin lowered into the grave with the name Norman Ruddock on the brass plate. As I stood there I thought that in years to come there will be another Norman Ruddock lowered into the grave, with another generation of Ruddocks present.

My father William was known as Willie, and he was fostered by a maiden aunt, Nellie, who lived in accommodation off the courthouse at the top of Rathdrum. She was Church of Ireland, and my father grew up in that tradition. In those days it was common for childless couples or spinster aunts to foster a child of a brother or sister. Because my father was brought up by a maiden aunt he was something of a stranger to his brothers and sisters.

The Ruddock grandparents moved about to various jobs. Grandfather did not like hard work, and I still remember his lily-white hands. Once, when I was preaching in Grangecon Church in Co Wicklow I was reminded of my grandmother who was sexton there, and would have polished the brass. They lived in a church cottage, which is now demolished. It was quite an experience for me to think of my grandmother who would have cleaned the church so many years before. Grandfather's job at Coolattin estate was not a very onerous one. He raised pheasants and watched out for poachers. He was also an authority on trees, and the estate was covered with trees. It was Charles Haughey, a former Taoiseach, who saved the last of the Coolattin oak woods from destruction. The Ruddock grandparents never owned a house, but sons Jack and Jim sent them money regularly. They also helped to pay for grandfather's one luxury, his pipe tobacco.

My first real memory of grandfather Ruddock was on a visit to Rathdrum. He lived in an old stone cottage behind the graveyard. It was an old outbuilding of the original rectory. I was in my twenties and an older brother and his wife had brought their first-born son to meet his great-grandparents. It was a moving moment as the old pair held their first great-grandchild, and we captured the historic event on camera. My grandfather was then over ninety and dressed in an immaculate black suit, white shirt and black tie. Always a careful dresser, he was especially well turned out that day. He was a tall, straight, imposing, and patrician figure with his pipe firmly clutched in his hand. He was a man of modest means, but his needs were simple. Grandfather seemed to me to be a quiet, gentle giant while grandmother was a strong, dominant, assertive woman who was talkative. My mother, her daughter-in-law, was also a strong personality, and there was a clash of temperaments. Like many a daughter-in-law, my mother was not fond of her mother-in-law.

My Father

I never knew my father, for when he died in 1938, I was only three years old. I sorely miss never having known a father's love, and I thank God that I was a father to my three daughters and a son. I was blessed to see them grow up from infancy to adulthood. Like his father before him, my father dressed well, whether formally with handkerchief in breast pocket, or less formally in sports jacket and flower in buttonhole. As the *Free Press* obituary said, 'He was a man with a sense of style who seemed to mix as easily with the county set as with the ordinary folk.' Father was regarded as the cleverest of his family, adept at figures and bookkeeping. That ability was recognised when he was appointed as office manager of William Armstrong of Enniscorthy, Co Wexford. Armstrongs were wholesale and provision merchants who had a fleet of orange-coloured vans on the road. On each side was the Armstrong logo – 'a strong arm'. These vans travelled all over the southeast. Many a time we waited at the forge beside Mrs Kenny's shop overlooking Ardamine, near Courtown Harbour, waiting for Armstrong's van to appear with a fresh supply of sweets. One of the highlights of our summer holidays at Ardamine were the regular visits to that old-world sweet shop of delicious smells.

My father would come home to Carlow most weekends by hired car, or ferried by his great cricketing friend, Jack Lett, of the old Enniscorthy brewing firm. The Lett's Brewery name is still preserved in France where you can still buy Lett's beer. It is a lovely nutty brown sweet beer. My father did drink, and he liked regular tots of Irish whiskey, but never to excess. He was not allowed bring his gundogs home, as my mother did not like animals. He lived with the misery of his daily bouts of asthma, the result of being gassed in the First World War. The medical aids available today for controlling asthma were not available in the hungry thirties. An old Huguenot man, who lived near my mother's ancestral home near Castledermot in Co Kildare, told me some years ago that when my father used to shoot with him, he would sit on the granite wall to catch his breath. In World War I, father had been a soldier in the North Irish Horse. Many Irishmen who fought in the British army were vilified, physically assaulted or snubbed when they returned home. Some rebels of

1916 despised these Irishmen who enlisted in the British army
while they themselves were in rebellion against the British.
There are stories of soldiers who fought in the British army
being attacked, and others boycotted. For decades the Irish gov-
ernment largely ignored the deaths of 60,000 Irishmen in the two
World Wars. The war memorial of Sir John Lutyens at
Islandbridge, near Dublin, lay derelict and abandoned. It was an
insult to those brave soldiers who died that we might live in
peace. It was heartening, some years ago, to see our own
President McAleese attend the unveiling of a memorial in
France to those brave soldiers. Queen Elizabeth, the President of
France and the German Chancellor were also present that day.
These Irish soldiers had finally been honoured.

On Sundays my father would go out shooting with friends,
and return with a brace of pheasant or snipe. He had developed
his own father's love of the gun. At Christmas time he would ex-
cite the family by laying a trail of gunpowder from a cartridge
along the floor, and then put a match to it. He loved lacing the
plum pudding with brandy and setting it alight. On one memorable occasion, he hired a Model T Ford and set off to visit his
parents in Rathdrum. The radiator had a leak and there were
regular stops for water. There was the geyser-like escape of
steam when father removed the radiator cap. Nobody in the
family can remember if the car ever reached its destination.

Cricket was my father's passion and a picture of Sir Don
Bradman, the Australian star, hung in our kitchen in Carlow. I
recently received an Australian gold dollar with Bradman's face
on one side. It reminds me of my father. The great Don lived into
his nineties and is looked on as a god in Australia. His son was
so tired of living in the shadow of his father's name that he
changed his name. However, he has now reverted to the name
Bradman. My father was known as Hobbs, after Sir Jack Hobbs
one of the immortals of English Test cricket. I can remember
being called Hobbs as a boy in Carlow. My father also loved or-
ganising boys' cricket matches during the summer months.

A month in the summer was spent in Ardamine, near
Courtown Harbour. My mother rented a chalet for five pounds a
month. We could have bought it for two hundred pounds. My
mother only came for part of the month as she had to look after

the shop in Carlow. Her sister Carrie acted as cook, housekeeper and childminder. One day when aunt Carrie was on the beach she watched my brother Charlie paddling his canoe. As a joke he turned his canoe over and she thought he was drowned. She nearly had a heart attack.

My mother had the terrible custom of throwing us into the sea, even though we could not swim. I was scared stiff of the water and I hid my bathing togs. My mother always went out to buy another. My mother loved the sea and would jump into the seawater no matter how cold it was. These were wonderful summers, as we built tunnels through the tall ferns beside the sand dunes. Much of this seaside area has been washed away by erosion and chalets have been destroyed.

My father saw very little of his children when they were growing up. He lived and worked in Enniscorthy and we were in Carlow. There must have been many tensions between my parents as my mother struggled to raise eight children and run a business. Luckily we had a live-in maid, Bridie, who was a substitute mother to us. She never missed daily Mass, and I remember when she came home from Mass she loved to have a rasher on toast for her breakfast. We had no proper bathroom at that time and she used to give each of us a bath in a zinc tub on Saturday evenings. Then Bridie would dry us in front of the warm Stanley range. Years later, my mother had a bathroom, dining room and extra bedroom built. I was heartbroken when my mother let Bridie go, as she had contracted tuberculosis. I remember the health inspector coming to our home to fumigate Bridie's bedroom. TB was a real scourge of the forties in Ireland until Dr Noel Browne, the Minister of Health, made great strides in eradicating the disease.

Most of my father's short life was lived as a married bachelor, away from home and family. Few people had cars, communications were difficult and few possessed phones. It was all a far cry from the mobile phone culture of today. My mother had ten children and two died in infancy. Most of us were delivered at home by a Nurse Smyth. I feel that by the time I arrived, my mother was tired of bearing children.

My father died on 30 May 1938. An obituary in the Carlow *Nationalist* of June 1938 read 'at the time of his death William

Edward Ruddock was manager and chief accountant at the head office of W. and S. Armstrong, Enniscorthy, and was extremely popular with the staff. He was in every sense a link between Carlow and Enniscorthy. Of a most urbane disposition, the late Mr Ruddock was held in high esteem by all who knew him.' The Wexford *Free Press* also carried news of my father's death – 'Sincere regret has been felt at the death of Mr W. E. Ruddock which occurred at his apartments, Main Street, Enniscorthy. He had been in failing health for some months but was only confined to bed for about ten days prior to his demise. Of a jovial and genial disposition, he was a favourite with people of every class.' He contracted pneumonia after a soaking at a local point-to-point and this, added to his chronic asthma, was too much for his frail body. My mother treasured the two half-crowns which were in my father's pocket when he died. Near the end of her life, my mother gave me my father's silver pocket watch. I had the watch repaired and brought it out to Australia to give to my own son. I have now lived twenty-eight years longer than my father. He lived such a short life.

My earliest memory in life was a visit to my father's grave some days after his funeral. I was three years and three months old and I remember the grave with a mass of flowers. I did not know what had happened and I did not understand. I remember being driven in a black car, though all cars were black in those days.

The Hungry Thirties

I was born on Monday 11 March 1935 and my father died on a Monday. I was born into an era of economic poverty, which was light years away from the affluence of today. The United States was recovering from the Wall Street Crash of the stock market and was in deep recession. Unemployment was high in Ireland and many Irish people took the emigrant boat. The Fianna Fáil Party, under its leader Éamon de Valera, was in power at my birth and pursued a Republican policy. De Valera wished to remove the oath of allegiance to the British Crown and promote industrialisation in Ireland. The Irish farmers had bought out their land from the landlords and were repaying the loans to the British government in London. These land annuities came to five million pounds a year, and de Valera decided to stop making these loan repayments. The British government replied by taxing imports of Irish cattle into Britain and the Free State replied by putting duties on British imported goods into Ireland. So began the economic war and Ireland suffered badly. It lasted about six years and finally, in 1938, the dispute was settled with a final payment of ten million pounds to the British government. As a result of this agreement the Irish ports were handed back to the Irish State by Britain.

This was also the era of travelling shows around Ireland. Michael MacLiammoir and Hilton Edwards put on Shakespeare and other plays around Ireland. So did MacLiammoir's brother-in-law, Anew McMaster. Other touring companies were led by Jimmy O'Dea and Maureen Potter. Later on Ronald Ibbs had a touring company and, when in boarding school in Kilkenny, we were sometimes allowed to attend the plays. Jack Doyle used to travel with Jimmy O'Dea. As well as being a flamboyant Irish heavyweight, Jack Doyle was an actor and singer with a great eye for the ladies. He was a very good-looking man. He was also fond of the bottle but he said that he was finished 'with the wild stuff'. He later went to Hollywood and married the film star Movita. That marriage did not last very long.

In the year of my birth, Dr Cullen, the Catholic bishop of Kildare and Leighlin, opened the new Barrow Milling Company with five other priests. Since pluralism was unheard of at this time, there was no thought of inviting the Church of Ireland bishop or rector. Minorities were considered of no consequence in the Irish State and were just about tolerated. An arrogant Catholic Church ruled supreme, and even the Irish government of the time was subject to it. The power of the Catholic Church was clearly shown when it forced the government to dump the radical and liberal Dr Noel Browne's mother and child scheme. The local paper wrote 'the lights of the mill blazed over the water, brilliant beacons of a returning hope'. This new mill was 'a new economic injection for Carlow'. With the rationalisation of the flour milling industry, this mill is now closed. How times have changed. At every opening of the Irish Sugar Company, the Catholic bishop was always present. Church of Ireland bishops hid behind the barricades, were never invited, or did not accept invitations. However, at the opening of a sugar facility in

Limerick, Walton Empey, Dean of Limerick, was present in robes. Walton later became my bishop in Meath and later still moved to Dublin as Archbishop. He was one who became very involved in community and civic life wherever he ministered. It was Pope John XXIII who opened the floodgates to ecumenism and held out the hand of friendship to other churches. He had a vision of a church based on love and not power.

In the 1930s, cinema came to Carlow when Tynan's Ballroom became the Ritz Cinema. It was a plush cinema and had a bar downstairs called the Buttery. The venture was the brainchild of Louis Elliman who owned cinemas in Dublin. It is now closed. During the 1940s, a second cinema was built in Carlow by the Pollard family. It was called the Coliseum and as we passed it on our way to school we watched the cinema being built, brick by brick. Each week, the posters for the two cinemas were displayed in my mother's shop and she received two complimentary tickets for both cinemas each week. My sisters and myself availed of these passes most Sundays. We would go to one cinema at three o'clock and the second at six o'clock. In those days the local cinemas showed two full-length films. The first film was often a cowboy and the second a thriller. I developed a great love for the cinema, and dreamed of being a cinema manager. The movie *Gone With The Wind* was booked out for weeks. Randolph Scott, Gene Autry, Roy Rogers and Gabby Hayes were my schoolboy heroes.

Cricket was very alive and well in almost every town and village in Ireland. It took the game a while to re-establish itself after the Second World War. Most of the estates of the landed gentry had their own teams, and their workers made up the eleven. Estates at Coolattin, Mount Juliet and Gowran Park all had teams. These places are now thriving golf clubs. When the estate system collapsed these cricket clubs died. Wexford is one of the few towns where cricket has survived, and they have to travel to Dublin for most matches.

Around 1949, I was picked up in boarding school and brought on an outing to Lismore where the Carlow team were due to play the local team. It was Lismore's first match after the war. This day out was a great treat as we drove through the Knockmealdown mountains. When we arrived at the Lismore cricket ground we saw the smouldering remains of the pavilion. It had been burnt the night before. Some blamed the local GAA and others lay the blame on the IRA. It was a vindictive action.

CHAPTER ONE

My Mother Emma

If I were drowned in the deepest sea
I know whose love would come down to me
Mother o'mine, mother o'mine.
Rudyard Kipling

My mother was born Emma Treacy on a small land-locked farm near Castledermot in the County Kildare. The land was poor and marshy and full of granite rock. The farm had a right of way to the main road along a narrow lane. Her parents lived to a ripe old age and mother's grandmother was a Jane Orthe from Germany. She had arrived with her sister in Ireland in the nineteenth century to find work. My mother was one of ten children, eight girls and two boys. Three sisters emigrated to England and two to the United States. My mother's brothers were bachelors and lived on the family farm. Sometimes I would cycle out to the farm with my mother when she would bring her brothers provisions and do their laundry. Once a month her brothers, Jack and Bill, would make an expedition to Castledermot in their pony and cart to stock up on supplies. Jack was a tall ascetic figure with a black beard while Bill was a little man who had been kicked by a horse and had suffered brain damage. He died suddenly in middle age in Naas hospital. Last year, I went to see the old farm, but the farmhouse had been razed to the ground and was now part of a giant field. Down an adjoining lane that day I met an old Huguenot man who had been a friend of my grandparents. He remembers my grandmother walking across the fields to church on Sunday afternoons. That day I gazed across the fields at the tower of the church.

My mother paid one visit to the United States to see her sister in Waterbury, Connecticut. Her American sister had not lost her Irish brogue. Her husband, also Irish, had not been to Ireland for forty years and wondered if there were still pigs in the kitchen. He could not believe that Irish roads were now tarred. It was a tearful farewell for the two sisters, as they knew that they would never see each other again in this life. My mother loved travelling and she enjoyed her visit to the new world. It was only in her later life she could afford to travel.

Ada was my mother's favourite sister and she was a companion to a wealthy lady in Farnham in Surrey. Mrs Hubband had once lived in Bray, Co Wicklow, where she married the local Church of Ireland curate. He never ministered again as he had married money, and ever after lived the life of a gentleman. As they say of men who marry wealthy women, he landed with 'his bum in the butter'! When my mother went to England to visit her sister, she was invited to share Mrs Hubband's pew in the front of the church. The servants sat in another pew at the back of the church. The cook took a shine to me and gave me money whenever I visited my aunt. When Mrs Hubband died the big house was sold. She left my aunt a charming cottage for the rest of her life. Ada was in every sense a refined lady, and extremely generous. When she came to Ireland she would take me out of boarding school for the day and lavish me with all kinds of goodies.

My mother probably met my father when he worked in Cope's shop in Castledermot. The shop is still there today. She was a beautiful young woman as her wedding photograph shows. She had a great business head, and she wrote with a beautiful script. She rented a small shop from the neighbouring landlord, W. G. Hadden, and we all lived over the shop. Space was cramped but we managed.

My mother's sister who lived near Carlow was childless, and she fostered a niece as a young girl. Ada was a very attractive young woman who had a job in Carlow. All hell broke loose when Ada was pregnant out of wedlock. She had fallen in love with a Catholic man, whom she later married. Ada was blamed for her aunt's sudden death shortly afterwards. Ada was unfortunately rejected for her behaviour, and my mother did not speak to her for years afterwards. This was a tragedy as Ada was a lovely woman and I lost contact with my first cousin.

My father's brothers and sisters all married Catholics, and their children were brought up as Catholics. These marriages caused a religious divide in our families and I grew up es-

tranged from all my first cousins. My mother was staunchly
Church of Ireland and did not approve of 'mixed marriages'.
'Mixed marriages' were not encouraged in the forties. Catholics
who wanted permission to marry someone outside their faith
had to give a written undertaking to bring up any children as
Catholics. This unjust rule decimated the non-Roman population in the state. These 'mixed marriages' generally took place
at a side-altar. I once attended the 'mixed marriage' wedding of
one of my pupils in the Pro Cathedral in Dublin, and this marriage took place at an obscure side-altar.

A book on Catholic dogma of the period has harsh things to
say about 'mixed marriages'. It writes of the evils of a 'mixed
marriage': 'The Church grants a dispensation for mixed marriage, but only for grave reasons and to avoid a greater evil. She
regards such unions with abhorrence, because they are hostile to
the spiritual good of the Catholic partner and the offspring, and
frequently lead to great unhappiness. Her dispensation is
grudgingly given, and does not remove the evil.' Later it goes
on: 'a Protestant is disqualified by his false belief from being of
any help to the Catholic partner or the children. He can never be
a help towards salvation, and he may be a grave hindrance.
Common sense tells us to avoid evil company. An honest man
who consorts with thieves may be dragged down to their level,
but something worse than this occurs in mixed marriage. The
children too are in the greatest danger of perversion.' We do not
now realise how far we have travelled from such a sectarian and
bigoted attitude. On the other hand I recall the Church of Ireland
businessman who had intended leaving his business to his long-
standing fellow churchman, who had worked for him for years.
When he announced that he was marrying a Catholic, he was
shown the door. A candidate for ordination in the Church of
Ireland was turned down because he was married to a Catholic.
When she died tragically, he was accepted for ordination. These
were bitter times, and we have travelled a long road to sanity.

Trinity College – Citadel of Satan?
When I was born in 1935 there was a controversy about County
Council university scholarships. The Roman Catholic bishops
were opposed to Catholic students attending Trinity College, as

it was looked on as a Protestant university that would corrupt
the minds of the faithful. A County Carlow councillor referring
to the Catholic bishop of Kildare and Leighlin stated that 'I accept without any reservation whatsoever the authority and
teaching of their lordships in this matter.' Catholic students with
County Council scholarships must study at the National
University while other denominations could attend Trinity
College. The National University was, however, open to all
creeds. Strangely enough I was never informed about these
scholarships. Here is an instance where I missed a father's guid-
ance and advice. These County Council scholarships were
means tested, based on Leaving Certificate results, and highly
competitive. The Catholic bishops' stance on this issue was a
feature of the times, and a clear example of the dogmatic power
that they exercised over their timid and subservient flock.

CHAPTER 2

Unwittingly to School

I began my education in 1939 at Barrack Street School, Carlow at the top of the town. It was called Barrack Street as it once had a British army barracks. The granite school had been endowed by the local Protestant landlords, the Browne-Claytons, who lived in a mansion at Browne's Hill. Their family crest was carved in stone on the front façade of the school. Our fairy godfather was the Church of Ireland rector, Archdeacon Samuel Ridgeway. He had large charitable funds at his disposal for education. Without help from these funds our family would never have received a secondary education. We were also blessed to have a fine principal teacher, Cecil Abbott. He gave up endless hours after school to prepare us for scholarships to various boarding schools. We all received scholarships, which virtually gave us a free education.

Cecil Abbott was no nine-to-three teacher. He was parish treasurer and took us on Tuesday evenings for the Young People's Union, known as the YPU. Here we played games and performed plays. Abbott also had a fine singing voice. One year I was cast as a babe in *Babes in the Woods*, with a little girl Anna who I had to sit with in the leaves.

Cecil Abbott used to take a children's choir. For some reason my friend Jimmy Restrick and myself were kicked out of the choir. Jimmy and I decided to sing in competition at the children's service in an upstairs box pew. We both sang loudly and, as we had strong voices, we drowned out the children's choir. We lived to regret that rebellious spirit because we had challenged the authority of Cecil Abbott, who I believe had kicked us out of the choir for singing too loudly!

The local Bank of Ireland agent's wife, Mrs Robertson, used to take four of us for singing lessons on Saturday mornings, and she never charged any fee. We were entered for the Féis Ceoil several years in Dublin. Pem Pollard, of the cinema family, who married the dashing curate Eric Stanley, continued to take me for singing and I always treasured that opportunity. I regret that I did not take up singing more seriously in adult life. Under Pem's tutelage I sang 'The Leprechaun' and 'Oh For the Wings of a Dove' at the Féis Ceoil in Dublin. One year the Féis coincided with the end of war festivities in Dublin in 1945. Some students at Trinity College hoisted the Union Jack over Front Square and it caused a riot outside the college walls. At the same time there was a wonderful military tattoo by the Irish army at the Royal Dublin Society to which I was brought. As one who spent hours dreaming up manoeuvres with toy soldiers, this display was one of the greatest thrills of my life.

Mrs Biddy Moore was the assistant teacher at Barrack Street National School and she had high blood pressure. She carried a cheap cardboard case to school and on her way home she would call to my mother's shop and tell her of any misdemeanours that we had committed. She was a real MI5.

There were dreadful toilets at the top of the yard, which were like the concentration camp toilets in the film *Schindler's List*. They always had a terrible smell. I was so nervous as a four-year-old that I wet my pants on the front steps of the school and I was very embarrassed and upset. These toilets were never updated during my primary schooldays. There was absolutely no investment in education in the forties. Primary schools were third world shacks with no visual aids, no proper heating or library. The teachers generally stood with their backsides to the fire while we shivered. Only the mittens saved us.

My best friend in national school was Jimmy Restrick. His father had a grocery shop in Dublin Street, beside the old Royal Hotel, now demolished. Our favourite snack at lunchtime was a packet of Bird's jelly, which was great value. Often on our way home from school we would visit Nanny Nolan's sweet shop and she had machines where you pulled a spring to release a lead ball which went round and round and entered various holes with different numbers. If you got a good score you won a token to exchange for sweets. Near her shop there were occasional fairs. We learned a lot about the facts of life when we saw a big stallion servicing a mare.

Jimmy and I were always up to some kind of devilment, but one of our unhappiest memories was the visit of a lady inspector to our class. She was strict and fussy and examined us all with difficult questions. Under my breath I called the inspector 'a bitch'. Biddy Moore, the teacher, asked what I had said. I sung dumb. Jimmy refused to inform on me. She kept us in for hours after school. Finally the inquisition ended, Jimmy folded and told the teacher what I had said. The palms of my hands were hot for a week! I cannot remember anything that Biddy Moore taught me except a poem:

Up the airy mountain, down the rushy glen,
We daren't go a-hunting for fear of little men.

Looking back, we had a happy childhood. Sometimes Jimmy and myself would take the old shop hand-truck and head out to the countryside looking for wood. In summer we swam at the weir on the river Burren above the town, or cycled out to a small river on the Athy road. At Christmas time my mother sent us out with an old blunt saw to search for a Christmas tree. Luckily we were not apprehended for trespassing. My mother had an artificial tree that she used each year in the shop window. Other times we visited Corcoran's mineral water factory, which had that lovely smell of bottling minerals. Whenever we called, we were given free lemonade. Corcoran's lemonade had a reddish colour and was sold all over the southeast of Ireland.

There was also the aromatic smell of the beet pulp during the sugar campaign from autumn to spring. On one occasion some of us in school were brought to the sugar factory to see sugar being made. It was fascinating. Now in 2005 the Carlow sugar factory is closing down on my birthday, 11 March.

George Bernard Shaw's mother Elizabeth Lucinda Gurly was born in Carlow, and Shaw inherited lands in the county. Shaw wrote of 'that cursed property in Carlow'. He also once wrote that Carlow was 'poor but proud'. If Carlow was poor, we never starved for my mother was an enterprising cook. I can still almost taste her lemon sponge puddings and apple dumplings. I can also remember the Sunday trifles and mashed potatoes baked in the Stanley oven with a lovely brown crust on top. Siphons of lemonade were treats on birthdays and at Christmas.

During World War II there were few luxuries, and chocolate was severely rationed. Grocers kept chocolate under the counter. Dark Dutch chocolate was available. There was no fruit. I used to mash parsnip with banana essence to create artificial bananas. There was great excitement when the war ended and fruit arrived. I went to the Atlantic Tea Company when I heard that dates had arrived. I was so disappointed when I saw dates, and when I tasted them. The grocery shops were all long-established chains of stores across the country – Leveret & Fry, Liptons, and the London & Newcastle. These shops have long-since gone, and impersonal supermarkets have taken their place.

We lived in a kind of ghetto community with little contact with our Catholic neighbours. We did not go near each others' churches, and Catholics had to get permission from their priests to enter Church of Ireland churches. It always intrigues me why thinking Catholics were so docile and subservient to their priests. We had a Protestant and Catholic gang as boys, and we had countless stone-throwing wars. I cannot remember any priest or religious leader enter our shop, though we had many good Catholic customers. I had never been inside the local Catholic church until I was an adult. We kept our heads down and almost apologised for not being 'papists'! There was dreadful religious apartheid. In my primary school there wasn't one Catholic on the roll. We were continually mocked for eating meat on a Friday. I could not see the fasting difference between a salmon and a sirloin steak. Everything closed down on Catholic Church holy days, and this seemed a hurtful injustice. There were no dances in Lent by order of the majority church, and cinemas were closed in Holy Week. Anne Small, the delightful owner of White's Hotel, told me the story of sitting in a Wexford church, and eight months pregnant. The priest lambasted the Smalls for running a dance in Lent. She felt insulted and humiliated. The following year the Catholic parish had a dance in Lent in the parish hall.

The Methodist Merchant
W. G. Hadden was the leading draper in Carlow town, with other shops in Wexford and Dungarvan. He was also a prominent Methodist in the local congregation. He lived in a fine

house overlooking the river Barrow on the Kilkenny road. He was a rigidly strict Methodist, and walked to work each day, arriving long before opening hours. Another Methodist, Billy Shaw, set up in the same street. Billy Shaw was an enterprising businessman, who sold his drapery goods at keen prices. Shaw eventually took over Hadden's, which is now part of Shaw's Almost Nationwide. One of Hadden's sons, who ran the business, died in middle age and his other son emigrated to Canada, where he too died in middle age.

Hadden employed Protestant apprentices wherever possible, and they came from all over Ireland. The apprentices were not allowed to smoke, had to be in by eleven at night, and were not allowed to go to the cinema or ride a bicycle on a Sunday. Their families had to pay Hadden a fee to serve an apprenticeship. They received ten shillings a month and their keep. It was alleged that when a messenger boy reached the age when his insurance card needed to be stamped, Hadden fired him. I earned valuable pocket money running errands for the shop assistants. Hadden's shop had a quaint system of sending money from the counter to the office. It travelled in a container run on a vacuum system. The container then returned some minutes later with receipt and change.

The YMCA was opposite Hadden's drapery store in Carlow. This was the social centre for the apprentices and here they played badminton, table tennis and billiards. There was a long dark passage down to the hall from the street. Here, shy farmers would grab at Hadden's virgins, but it was all innocent. I could not understand why a light was never put in the passageway.

My mother's rent was minimal and each week payment was registered in a cashbook. When we had left home, Hadden tried to get possession of my mother's shop and home, as he was the landlord. He would give my mother five hundred pounds if she would sign over the property. Hadden pestered my mother to move, and it caused her distress. She was no fool, and refused to sign. Hadden realised that my mother had no intention of moving, and that he had no chance of possession. He then sold her the lease, and she was able to sell the shop. This enabled her to buy a comfortable home in Dublin. For the first time in her life she had her own home and garden. She loved flowers and plants, and in Dublin she spent some happy years until her death in 1975. She was tired of shop keeping and the shop had become too busy for her busy as the town grew.

The daily round

Delivering newspapers was one of the daily tasks of my childhood. Newspapers were delivered free to every house until a sixpence weekly charge was introduced. I had my round to do each morning before school. When it was windy and raining it was almost impossible to keep the papers dry. After school the English papers and the evening papers had to be delivered. These papers had to be collected at the station from the afternoon train. The sale of evening newspapers fell away sharply, and dwindled to nothing. Getting to school on time after a paper round was always a tight schedule, and sometimes I was caned for being late.

At Christmas some of our customers gave us money and gifts for their paper delivery. One of the kindest customers was Mrs Governey of the shoe factory family. She always wore black and laced leggings. She was every inch a lady. The shoe factory was opposite the mineral water complex, and there was a lovely smell of leather as I passed it. The shoe workers marched down the town each morning, and their hobnailed boots made a great noise. They were often whistling and singing. At six in the evening the hooter sounded, and they all marched home again. Governey's boots were famous, but the factory is long since closed.

When I delivered newspapers to the rectory I would always ring the bell long and loudly. If the then rector or his wife arrived at the door, I would always get a slice of cake or a piece of fruit. It was heaven. On one occasion, with my brother Reg, I spent several days hanging cheap prints for a new incoming rector. I didn't receive even a cup of tea, and the new broom gave out no cake or fruit!

Once a week, generally on a Monday, I sometimes brought the week's lodgement to the AIB – it was then the Provincial Bank. Sometimes the lodgements were small, and they would swell at Christmas, or when people paid their monthly bills. One cleric only paid his bill once a year. I remember my mother coming back from the bank in tears, because her account was overdrawn. In those days there were no overdrafts. Bank managers were like gods.

My mother's tears were evident one Christmas Day. Next door lived a Presbyterian couple, a Mr and Mrs Gibson. He worked next door in Hadden's. She was positively unfriendly, and never spoke to us. The Gibsons were 'Orange Northerners', and one Christmas Day I threw dirty loo paper across the boundary wall. Our neighbours called the guards, and my mother was upset. It was a stupid thing to do. On the twelfth of July, the Orangemen's Day, I always hoisted a tricolour for our neighbours to see.

Two other memories of my childhood are very clear. One was the launching of the big barges by Thomas Thompson Engineering Works. These barges were used to carry sugar and other goods on the Barrow navigation system. We got off school early to watch the launching of the barges. While the barges were slow, it was a very easy way to transport goods, and they took traffic off the roads.

Another memory was the point-to-point races at Kellistown, near Carlow. This was one of the highlights of community life, and school finished early. One race day, Count John McCormack, the distinguished Irish tenor, was down to sing at the Ritz cinema in Carlow. McCormack sang to an almost empty house, and he vowed that he would never sing in Carlow again. He never did.

My mother was a very organised woman. She did her washing on Monday, ironing on a Tuesday, cleaned the house from top to bottom on Wednesday. On Thursdays she sent out the bills, and addressed copies of *The Carlow Nationalist* to destinations all over the world. One or two years she got the contract to sell programmes at the revived Carlow Show. This was a very profitable venture, and we got generous payment for selling all day long. Her hobbies were playing whist and cycling out to the country to visit friends. She loved Jimmy O'Dea and Maureen Potter, and rarely missed a pantomime. Jimmy O'Dea came regularly to the Town Hall in Carlow to put on variety shows.

The rowing club had a good supply of rowing boats and, as members of the club, we could book a boat for the day. We would row up the river as far as Knockbeg College, where there was a lovely picnic spot beside the weir. To go further upriver or downriver involved passing through tedious locks so we did not travel far.

The Venerable Archdeacon Samuel Ridgeway was the formidable rector of Carlow and he had a very gravelly voice. He would cycle into the town on an upstairs bicycle with bicycle clips in place. His bark was worse than his bite. Meeting an old lady, Mrs Hennessy, in the street, he asked her to account for her absence from public worship. 'Be there next Sunday', he barked. He wouldn't get away with it now. When a nervous curate, the Revd Adrian Fisher, celebrated Holy Communion for the first time as a priest, the Archdeacon shouted across the sanctuary: 'You forgot the Creed, you fool!' I was there. We loved to see the curates coming into school as it brought variety. They numbered the posh and aloof, Neville Phair, the bishop's son, a Revd Daunt from Cork, who was a real character and used to bring us on trips up the hills. One day he brought us in autumn to a hazelnut wood in the Killeshin hills where we picked nuts. Another curate, Eric Stanley, later Archdeacon of Killaloe, was a real hands-on person, who took us for hockey. The last curate of my youth was Dr Rex Reynolds from South Africa, a man not cut out for parish life. On one occasion he called in the morning to visit a farmer's wife, Mrs Switzer, who was feeding the pigs when he arrived. She carried two buckets of pig swill. She didn't know what to do. 'You know, Dr Reynolds', she said, 'if you had come an hour later you could have had lunch with me.' 'Oh not at all', Dr Rex replied, 'a cup of tea will do!' Rex was a kindly man though, and took me for Latin grinds for 'littlego'. This was an exam in Trinity College at the end of second year which every student had to pass.

A Real Saint

The most influential cleric of them all was Precentor Jack Nelson, who was rector of a nearby country parish for over forty years. He was a wonderful preacher and a kind gentleman. I regularly cycled out to his rectory to help in the garden, and especially in summer and autumn to harvest the fruit. On one occasion I cycled out to his rectory to pick apples. All I had to wear was an old torn pair of cricket trousers. Next morning he was in to my mother with a cheque to buy me a new pair of pants. I rarely had new shoes or clothes, but wore my brother's cast-offs. On another occasion, I ate more raspberries than I picked and I was sick. On leaving for secondary school, he gave me a prayer book and told me 'to play hard and pray hard'. I may have played hard, but not prayed hard. He was a kind of father that I never had. He preached at my ordination to the priesthood in St Canice's Cathedral, Kilkenny. On news of his death I wept bitterly. He was the clergyman who fostered my vocation. He had a great love for people. When he died his widow wrote to me of her husband. She wrote, 'Whenever he looked at the stars his thoughts flew heavenward.' He could be earthy too. Once, when visitors gave him money for looking up ancestors, he told the visitor that he would give the money to Protestant orphans. Later he said, 'I'm a Protestant orphan!' and put the money in his pocket! Though a very humble man, Jack always wanted to be a Canon of St Patrick's Cathedral, which was the gift of the bishop. However, a younger cleric was always licking up to the bishop, spoke with a cultivated accent, and got the job. Precentor always reminded me of Precentor Nelson. When our present bishop invited me to become Precentor of the Chapter of Ferns Cathedral, I believe that Jack Nelson would have been pleased. The Precentor in a Cathedral is responsible for the music, and is the senior member of the Chapter next to the Dean. It is the Precentor who installs a new Dean.

The Sound of the Willow

Golf was an exclusive game in my childhood, and only played by the gentry and the quality. Cricket began to be played again after the Second World War. It was looked on as a foreign game. My mother loved cricket, which may be due to my father's influence. She was the official scorer to the Carlow Cricket Club, and she wrote in her meticulous neat script.

The Australian cricket team that toured England in 1948 was a mighty team. It was captained by Sir Donald Bradman who was making his last tour. He was bowled for a 'duck' in his last test match outing at the Oval cricket ground in London. It was a team of brilliant test stars, including Ray Lindwall, fast bowler, and Keith Miller, all rounder. A Carlow Cricket enthusiast, Sammy Roche, a solicitor, was visiting England for the tests, and happened to be staying in the same hotel as the Australians. He invited them to visit his lovely home, near Carlow. Lindsay Hassett, vice-captain, and former test stars Bill O'Reilly and Jack Fingleton, arrived in Ireland to great excitement. A practice was arranged with some of the local cricketers. They found ace bowler Bill O'Reilly, almost unplayable.

My mother prepared the cricket teas for each home match at the mental hospital grounds. The hospital chapel stood beside the cricket ground and on one occasion J. P. Fellows-Smith of Oxford University hit a six right over the church roof. He afterwards played for his native South Africa. When my mother died, an editorial wrote of 'the end of an innings'.

CHAPTER 3

The Murder Machine

My childhood was coming to an end and, in the summer of 1947, I was living in fear of going to boarding school in Kilkenny College. I had done well in the scholarship exam and, with the assistance of a local bursary, the Browne Fund, I had a virtually free secondary education. I spent a good deal of the summer building a wooden tuck box, as the food was poor in Kilkenny. I collected a good supply of chocolate over the summer to keep the wolf from the door, and I stored it in my tuck box, along with other goodies. It was essential to have a lock on the tuck box, as not all boys were honest.

On my first day I travelled to Kilkenny on the train with my mother, where I met the imposing figure of Corrodius Gilbert Shankey, the headmaster. He had qualified as an engineer, and had come to Kilkenny as a temporary teacher twenty-five years previously. He had never left.

The junior boys lived in John Street House, across the street from the main school. Those who arrived early got the best beds. There was no hot water or central heating, and in winter it was not unlike the Gulag camps in Siberia. The cold water for washing was kept in enamel jugs and, in winter, the ice was frozen solid on top of the water. Consequently, we did not wash often in winter. Four years later, the headmaster announced that he was installing 'hot showers for the boys'. Before the advent of showers, there was a bath once a week on a Saturday evening. The water was heated by an antique boiler in the 'boot' room, fed with coal. The hot water was severely rationed, and there was first bath, second bath or third bath, in the same bath water. If one was unlucky enough to be on third bath, the water was a dirty brown colour, and disgusting. Prefects supervised the baths, and some of them enjoyed the sight of the procession of nude boys.

Our tuck boxes were stored in the 'boot' room, and needed to be padlocked at all times. I would have starved to death without tuck. The food was Spartan, bread and margarine for breakfast, a fair lunch, and bread and butter for supper. Once a week we got sausages and fried potato for supper, and on another evening, jam tart. On Sunday mornings there was revolting German sausage, and marmalade was a treat. Each week we received a ration of two ounces of butter and margarine. It was post-war margarine, more akin to grease, and I never ate it. My mother sent me regular supplies of country butter. The dining room was full of ants in the summer, and we had to knock ants out of the bread. A dead mouse was discovered in the bread one day, and I don't know why we didn't sue the baker. We were served yesterday's bread so that we did not eat too much. The baker probably sold the bread cheaply to the school. One of the worst customs was serving tea in big enamel pots, already mixed with the milk. It was a disgusting drink, and the object of the exercise was to economise on the milk. No wonder we got bad teeth! One concession was boiled eggs. If you brought your own eggs, the kitchen staff would boil them. I was not the first boy to complain in adult life that the food ruined our health, and I, like some other boys, developed stomach ulcers. I can remember having a pain in my stomach from the hunger.

There were many complaints about cold beef, which was served twice a week. As a prefect, I was one of a deputation that went to see the headmaster to complain about cold beef in winter. He nearly blew his top, but finally decided to put hot rabbit on the menu instead. One day, as I looked out a classroom window, I saw a maid with a zinc bath full of skinned rabbits. She was draining blood out of the bath into the dirty drain outside the kitchen door. Several of the rabbits fell into the drain, and she simply threw them back in the bath again. The rabbits were served head and all, and a teacher at the head of the table said that the head was the tastiest part of the rabbit! I could never eat rabbit again.

I missed freedom more than anything else in boarding school. Leaving the school premises was forbidden, and we were barred from visiting nearby shops. There was a school tuck shop, and it was first port of call when money arrived in the post. Some boys pinched apples from the headmaster's garden,

but it was a dangerous pastime. One boy from Co Wexford regularly received parcels of sweets and chocolate. I remember he
would tease us with Rowntree's Fruit Gums. If we guessed the
right colour of the next gum out of the packet, he would part
with it. I never guessed the right colour. He was totally selfish,
and never shared his sweets with anyone else. I remembered
these incidents recently when I saw his death in the paper.

Sombre Sundays
On Sundays, first and second year boys wore a black jacket,
striped trousers, white shirt, black tie, and Eton collar. I had to
carry a mortarboard to church. Third form upwards wore a
black suit, white shirt and black tie. Before moving off in croco-
dile to St John's Church across the road, we had to line up, and
the headmaster walked down the line inspecting our dress.
Some of us sang in the Cathedral Choir each Sunday, and we
had the freedom to walk up the city. On the last Sunday of the
school year, boys who were leaving threw their mortarboards
and school caps over the bridge into the river Nore.
    On Sunday evenings, we went to evensong at St Mary's
Church where Dr George Seaver, the Dean, spoke to us. Dr
Seaver was a literary giant, and we were delighted when he was
awarded a Doctorate of Literature by Trinity College. We were
proud to see him wear his red and blue academic hood. He had
come to Ireland from England as Dean's Vicar of St Canice's
Cathedral, Kilkenny. When the Deanery of Ossory was vacant, it
was felt by some that he would not be suitable, as he had no
wife. However, justice prevailed and he was appointed. Seaver
was a very good-looking man with silvery white hair. He wrote
many books, including biographies of Schweitzer and
Archbishop Gregg of Armagh. A request was sent to Dean
Seaver that the boys wished to hear him speak every Sunday
evening. He was a priceless storyteller, and he captivated us
with his stories of Scott, Wilson and Shackleton of the Antarctic,
and of Albert Schweitzer's exploits in Africa. He had an engag-
ing stutter. Seaver was one who first encouraged me to think of
ordination. On the day of his installation as Dean of St Canice's
Cathdral, he came over to me in the choir stalls and said that I
might be Dean one day. That was not to be.

The headmaster, Shankey, did not suffer fools gladly. He was a science teacher and, when a boy accidentally poured mercury down the sink, he almost exploded with anger. He was known as 'Shal' because on Sundays he took Bible classes, and spoke to us of King Shalmanezer. Shankey was a fine scripture teacher and he brought the Old Testament to life. We used to sit a Church of Ireland Synod Exam. The results and names of all the pupils across Ireland were published in a booklet. It was a terrible custom, especially if you got bad marks. People from Cork to Coleraine could read your results, and the headmaster conducted a post-mortem of the results. One day a Tipperary boy shouted 'Hooray for Shal' as he left the schoolroom. Shankey heard. 'Who said that?', he said. 'Come with me.' The boy had ridges on his backside for months afterwards, and the nurse rubbed ointment on his bottom daily. Today he would be up in court. On another occasion, his wild eldest son spat on the floor. When the headmaster arrived to take morning roll call he saw the spit. 'Whoever spat on the floor was born in a pigsty!' he shouted.

Headmaster Shankey used to take off on occasional weekends to see his daughter Maeve play hockey for Ireland. As well as being a fine athlete, she was a fine looking woman. We would always know when Shankey was leaving, as the workman Johnny was detailed to wash his Ford Mercury car. When the headmaster was away, the Maths teacher Richard Hendy was in charge. Hendy addressed us one Sunday morning with these words, 'By the power delegated to me by the headmaster, I am the acting headmaster, and I have complete power!'

Some boys swam in the River Nore when the medical officer had banned swimming due to pollution in the river. All hell broke loose on Monday morning. The headmaster, with 'Dick Hendy' at his side, addressed the school assembly. 'We hold all the aces, don't we Mr Hendy?' the headmaster roared. 'Quite right, Mr Headmaster, we hold all the aces', Hendy replied. The boys who swam were suspended, and it was alleged that the head never gave them references on leaving school.

Prison Camp

As preparation for marking pitches, the grass sod was turned to make a line – no white line was used. We boys had to walk up and down the line for days, compacting the sods. We were like a chain gang, with prefects supervising the work.

I loved hockey but hated playing rugby, as I was small. Rugby was compulsory. Hockey was one of the bonuses of school, and when I was picked on a team we got trips to play in Waterford and Dublin. We played in one cup final in Dublin and stayed overnight. We were delighted to win that trophy. Later, I was appointed school hockey captain by Richard Hendy, who was the coach. Dick Hendy was a fine teacher. We had some terrible junior teachers at Kilkenny, but Hendy redressed the balance. He was also a keen fisherman, along with his wife 'Polly'. He drove a baby Ford. When it was laid up during the war, boys poured sugar into the petrol tank, and God knows what else. Sometimes he would invite us up to tea. His wife baked delicious cream and jam sponge cakes.

The headmaster used to have school exams on public holidays such as St Patrick's Day. We revolted on one occasion – we went on strike and marched down to the bog in front of the school. That ended public holiday exams.

There was a rigid class system. First year boys couldn't enter a second form room, and second year boys couldn't enter a third form room. There was the terrible punishment of 'screwing' – a junior boy would have a senior boy put his arm around his head, and tighten until the younger boy screamed. Bullying was par for the course. One fat boy from Co Offaly was so abused by bullies, both verbally and physically, that he tried to hang himself on the stairs. He did not complete his schooldays. The same boy received a big barm brack one Halloween. He was told that it had coins inside it, he pulled it apart, gave it to us, and told us that all he wanted were the coins!

On one occasion, a lovely old couple from Malahide, County Dublin, friends of a brother of mine, arrived at the school to see me. They gave me a huge bag of bananas and a monster bag of sweets. It was like heaven. I shall never forget the kindness of Frank and Kitty Manning that day.

I was a choirboy in St Canice's Cathedral and sometimes my local rector, Archdeacon Ridgeway, would arrive to preach. He also came to the school for board meetings. He would pull out his purse and give me a shilling. It was like a fortune. He always remembered to look for his poor parishioners from Carlow. My brother Charlie was in the Royal Navy, and he sent me postal orders regularly throughout my schooldays. Another benefactor was Joe, an old friend of mine from Castlecomer. Joe was a postman and one of the gentlest men that I have ever known. He also sent me postal orders, and sometimes brought me to see the Kilkenny hurling team play at Nowlan Park. I remember the excitement of seeing Christy Ring, Jim Langton and Terry Leahy playing. Those games gave me a great love of hurling. Joe was also a keen river fisherman and taught me how to fish. When I drive through Castlecomer I sometimes stop to visit Joe's grave in the church grounds.

Hopping Hormones
Kilkenny College, in my time there, was a citadel of repressed sexuality and abuse. I suppose that this is only natural in a repressive boys' school. Now that the college is coeducational, and operating in an enlightened environment, it bears little relationship to what we experienced fifty years ago. In my time, the headmaster decided to take in a token number of girls, which included his younger daughter and two Kilkenny girls. Strangely enough, none of the boys had a crush on any of them.

One of the worst customs in boarding school was the rite of initiation. New boys were called 'grabbers' and, after lights out, the new boys had to run naked down the dormitory while the seniors beat them with soap wrapped in wet towels. Masturbation was a physical relief to boys who were bored. Once a year, a clergyman from a missionary society used to visit the school to talk to us about sex. Masturbation was his key theme, and he spoke about its evil, and how it could lead to blindness! I felt that this cleric had a fierce hang-up on sex. The same cleric ran summer camps, but I had no desire to be further indoctrinated about the evils of masturbation.

Younger boys, especially the pretty ones, were always in danger of the senior 'studs'. The pretty boys were given feminine nicknames. Nicknames were also abusive and cruel. Fat boys were called 'fatty', 'porky' or 'fatso'. A boy with a limp was called 'hopalong'. I was called 'Mr Dean' because I went to early communion in the cathedral.

Wet days were a trial, and there wasn't a decent book to read in the library. These were pre-television days, and an old radio was our only contact with the outside world. On rugby international days the newspapers printed a drawing of the ground, so that we could follow the areas of play on the radio. Sitting around a big stove in the schoolroom was another pastime on wet days.

There were some poor teachers at Kilkenny and some brilliant ones. Richard Hendy was a fine Maths and Art teacher. Kingsley Scott was a brilliant English teacher who imbued me with a great love of the English language. He was a debonair man, and a free thinker in a centre of conservative orthodoxy. The Latin teacher, Frank Lipsett, prided himself on getting higher marks in university than the Greek scholar, W. B. Stanford, former professor at Trinity College. Lipsett was a very moody man who was eccentric, and he had a vicious temper. One day he hit a boy and literally knocked him out. The boy's nose bled for hours. Lipsett only married in middle age and there was secret laughter in prep when we noticed that he was reading a book on the anatomy of sex.

The main Irish teacher was a man named Fred Rea. He was known as 'Biff' Rea because he had been a member of the boxing club at Trinity College. He had the habit of punching one fist into the palm of the other. 'Biff' had high blood pressure, and was not the best of disciplinarians. However, he was not a teacher to fool around with due to his boxing prowess. The school also employed a number of student teachers, who had little experience of teaching. It showed.

One of the most exciting events was the arrival of a female French teacher, who had graduated from University College, Cork. Lucy O'Callaghan hailed from Cork, and she had a beautiful melodious voice. Lucy was a very attractive looking woman, and a very good teacher of French. I was very interested in French and she used to take me after school for phonetic lessons, which was very decent of her. Here I had this lovely creature to myself for a whole hour after school! Lucy was also a very smart dresser, and wore provocative see-through jumpers. She had captivating breasts. I suppose that she was the first woman that I 'fell in love with'! In class Lucy wore short tight skirts and, when she sat at the high teacher's desk, we could see her knickers. She would blush with embarrassment as we whispered 'blanc aujourdhui, rouge aujourdhui, bleu aujourdhui' (white today, red today, blue today)! She was very patient, and I suppose that we were only confirming her femininity. I only met her once in life afterwards, when we bumped into each other in a Dublin restaurant. She must be an old lady now, but for me she will always be a vibrant young woman.

The school nurse was Blanche Rathwell from Ballycanew in Co Wexford. She was a most kind and attractive woman who spent most of her adult life in Kilkenny College. She had a number of romances with bachelor teachers, but marriage never happened. I came across Blanche in Wexford hospital, where I was chaplain, some weeks before she died. As her parish had no priest at the time, her family invited me to take her funeral. I was privileged to do so, and I was very moved, as I had known her for over fifty years. When Blanche treated my pains and aches in school, little did I realise that I would be with her at the end of her mortal life.

Gym in the broken down ball alley was a real purgatory. It was taken by a sadistic army sergeant. I was terrified as I couldn't jump over the high wooden horse. Eventually, the leaking ball alley was replaced with the George Berkeley Hall which was opened by R. M. Smylie, the swashbuckling and dynamic editor of *The Irish Times*. Berkeley, the eminent philosopher and Bishop of Cloyne, was one of Kilkenny's most famous past pupils. Dean Jonathan Swift, Congreve, and Admiral Beatty were others. Beatty hailed from Co Wexford and was known as 'the ram' in the navy as he had a weakness for women. He always wore his peaked cap at an angle as a sign of individuality.

The headmaster had the tradition of giving out state intermediate numbers to the boys several days before the exam. We sat the exam in the Christian Brothers School. We felt great freedom as we walked up the town, as we were rarely allowed outside the school gates. One boy, who did not receive an exam number, put up his hand, 'I didn't receive a number sir.' The head laughed sarcastically, 'You, you don't think you're sitting the exam. You can wait until next year.' That was judge and jury, and I'm sure that parents today wouldn't accept that kind of dictatorial treatment. I felt deeply for that boy that morning as he was a close friend of mine in school, and a hard, industrious worker. I believe that he would have had no problems passing the intermediate certificate.

One of the great characters in Kilkenny was a man called Stallard who owned a cinema near the Club House Hotel. One evening, when he had a good quantity of alcohol on board, he arrived at the headmaster's door. *The Best Years of Your Life*, a post-war film, was showing at his cinema, and he wanted to give all the boys a free show. He would not budge until Shankey agreed to let us go. That was a wonderful event. On several other occasions he gave us free tickets to several of Ronald Ibbs and Anew McMaster's plays. Stallard, I believe, owned Archersfield, which we used as our playing fields. It is now a mass of houses.

Au Revoir

Kilkenny College was, in 1951, only a four-year cycle school, and boys generally went on to Mountjoy School in Dublin to complete the six-year cycle. My last day in Kilkenny was a sad day, and I would miss most of all early morning worship in the side chapel at St Canice's Cathedral. A group of us went there most Sunday mornings for early communion at eight. The stained glass window in the side chapel remains vividly in my memory. It was of a crusader, kneeling in prayer, in preparation for the battle ahead. The last day at Kilkenny brought about a new air of freedom as parents arrived for sports day, and luggage was packed into motorcars bound for places as far away as Cork and Kerry. In front of the school, the prizes were presented by the bishop, John Percy Phair. He was the expert of the dramatic pause. Turning towards the school, he said, 'I love these hallowed walls.' It was inside these walls that the headmaster and the bishop roared and swore over their billiard games. One sports event stands out in my memory. Some boys had noticed that the third prize in the mile race was a beautiful Swiss penknife. It was quite funny as all the runners tried to come in third rather than win cheap EPNS and bronze medals, which were the first and second prizes.

The head prefect hailed from Co Wexford, and would have

been well suited as a commandant of a concentration camp. I watched one day as a senior boy from Co Carlow made as if to kick one of the teachers in the backside. The head prefect saw him and administered the most savage beating, with innumerable belts of a pliable tennis shoe on his behind. The prefect had a foul temper, and dealt out punishment in a fit of great anger. That boy, who had been so brutally punished, went out afterwards to meet family visitors. People have no conception of the levels of cruelty in boarding schools in the forties. The head prefect never smiled, never talked to any of us, and meted out punishment monotonously. Punishment in the winter months was doled out with a hockey stick, or tennis shoe. The tennis shoe was unbelievably painful. In summer the cricket bat was the traditional tool of terror. Nobody shouted 'Stop!' in a so-called Christian school, and the teachers did not know what was going on.

However, treachery returns to the treacherous one. I happened to be present outside on sports day, and I watched the head prefect standing beside the school bell. Suddenly, from the top window, I saw a boy holding a laden chamber pot, filled by many of us. He proceeded to pour it down on the head prefect. The aerodynamics were perfect, because it hit the target spot on. Turning on his heels, the head prefect raced up the stairs in a foul temper, but he never discovered the culprit. Anything can happen on a sports day, and there is no opportunity for inquests, as everyone was going home. I was never as happy to see a brutal prefect get a dose of his own medicine. It was a harsh and degrading act, and portrayed how unpopular he had been.

My final sports day arrived. I had picked up a good few prizes, including the Mayne Cup, which goes to the boy who made the most of his time at school. The headmaster bid me goodbye, and thanked me for my industry as a pupil. He wished me well. I would only see him once again in a Dublin hospital where I was chaplain. C. G. Shankey retired to Howth where he dropped dead, out walking his dog. Shankey was a great walker who kept very fit. He had been a fine athlete and rugby player in his younger days. All his children were fine athletes.

Kilkenny is now a changed place. John's House, where I slept as a junior, is now a garden shop. The old site of Kilkenny

College is now the headquarters of Kilkenny County Council. The Berkeley Hall is now history. The County Council has built a hideous atrium on to the Georgian school building. That kitchen drain where the maid drained the blood from the rabbits is no more. Various memories flood in upon me when I visit the old college site. It is amazing to see hundreds of years of school history bite the dust, with the sale of the buildings and grounds. However, a new school with substantial grounds stands on a new site. It is a pity that the names of two fine teachers, C. G. Shankey and R. Hendy who gave their whole life to the college, did not have new buildings named after them.

It is now fifty-three years since I left Kilkenny College for the last time. That summer of 1951 was to be my last summer of ease. I played cricket on the local team, and we travelled all over the Southeast to play opposing teams. A visit to Wexford Cricket Club that summer reminds me of the century scored that day by a schoolboy, Séamus Kelly, then a schoolboy at Clongowes Wood College in Co Kildare. Séamus played rugby for Ireland later on. Another Co Wexford native was Bill Tector from Clonroche who taught me at Kilkenny, and who also played rugby for Ireland. He was a fine athlete. When I was rector of Bill's home parish, he would always call when down on holiday. Bill was a great encourager who died too young of cancer.

CHAPTER 4

One Flew Over the Cuckoo's Nest

The movie with the brilliant Jack Nicholson as the antihero takes us to a psychiatric nursing home in the United States. Nicholson playing the part of Mac Murphy is a rebel to authority and institutionalism. He continually challenges authority, and his punishment is heavy sedation and finally horrific electric shock treatment and death. The late Dr Noel Browne wrote in his autobiography, *Against the Tide,* that shock treatment was the most bestial crime committed on another. At one point in the movie Mac Murphy leads all the inmates out of the nursing home, loads them on to a vacant bus, and takes them on a trip. For the first time in years they experience freedom and the joy of adventure. However, they are all soon incarcerated again and continue a vegetable like existence for the rest of their mortal journey.

My own depression I believe began when I was sexually abused as a twelve-year-old boy. That depression lived with me throughout my teenage years. These depressed feelings were too awful to deal with, and were locked inside. Hence the depression.

Some say that depression is repressed anger and I was certainly angry when I recalled my own abuse. However, that very experience has helped me to help others. Depression is a disease of our time. When I resigned my Co Wexford parish and helped to run a bookshop in Killarney, the books on depression 'flew out the door'. We could never keep enough of them in stock. Depression is also genetic, and seems to pass on from one generation to another. I live with the fear that I may have passed on the depression to my own children. I hope not.

Depression may also be environmental and may be caused by a poor marriage, an unhappy work environment or a lack of self-confidence and self esteem. Depression is the long dark night of the soul. He or she loses interest in everything, work, family and even life itself. There is no desire to get up in the morning and a real desire to draw further into oneself. Drugs may help but they do not deal with the root cause. It is impossible to imagine what it is like unless you experience it.

On one occasion a friend of mine came to visit. He is a distinguished academic in his own school with a brilliant record of university achievement. As we walked along the road, he began to weep and he shared how he found it impossible to face a class for lectures as he had lost all confidence. He was clinically depressed. He however recognised his need, sought help, and is now living a normal life. Recently we met again and talked of his experience. It is uplifting to see people come through the eye of the storm.

My lifeline was a parishioner who also suffered from depression. Through much time spent with a psychotherapist he is now living a normal life. Changing jobs and life style have transformed him. One summer's evening outside the church my friend pleaded with me to go and see Professor Norman Moore, the godfather of Irish psychiatry, and an authority on Dean Jonathan Swift. Professor Moore was the clinical director of St Patrick's Hospital in Dublin which was founded by Jonathan Swift. Over the front door are the telling words – 'Festina Lente', 'hasten slowly'

Norman Moore assessed that I was a cyclothymic manic-depressive – basically a mild form. Some of the greatest geniuses in the world have been manic depressives, Winston Churchill, Prime Minister, John Ogden Pianist, Composers Beethoven and Tchaikovsky to name a few. Professor Moore advised me to get involved, get my hands in the soil. As an expert gardener he found great contentment with his hands in the soil. It is certainly true and I am once again developing a keen interest in the garden. A self-confessed alcoholic relative gave me three words of comfort which I have never forgotten – 'it will pass'. The depressive stage of my life has now passed, though I am continually having to deal with repressed anger which at times erupts like an unsettled volcano, and upsets those closest to my heart. I am aware of the problem and am dealing with it. I am blessed and feeling on top of the world. A great friend and counsellor was a parishioner of mine in Co Westmeath, Dr Marie McKeon, a psychiatrist. She died too young of a tumour on the brain. Marie had a wonderful listening ear and loads of common sense. She helped me to understand myself better, and to journey onwards without excess baggage.

For most of my adult life my wife Jean has had to cope with my bouts of depression. It has not been easy for her, but she had helped me to take on board self acceptance and to begin loving myself. It is the sensation of being in the pit or 'the well of despond' as John Bunyan wrote in *The Pilgrim's Progress*. I used to feel so impotent, not wanting to get up in the morning, and losing all interest in everything around me. Now that long dark night has passed, and I feel on top of the world, and longing to live every minute with which life presents me.

CHAPTER 5

Dublin

In Dublin's fair city where the girls are so pretty

A farmer's wife believed that the Dubliners went down to Kingsbridge Station to laugh at the culchies getting off the train. She was quite an intelligent Wexford woman and I could not take her seriously. I felt like a culchie arriving for my first day at Mountjoy School. I took my battered old bicycle off the train, and tied my two suitcases on the bike, one on the back carrier and the other tied to the lamp holder on the front. I cycled from Kingsbridge to the school which must have been about ten miles. In hindsight I should have taken a taxi, but that would have been a financial luxury. When I arrived at the school I discovered that I had arrived a day late. However, Mountjoy was a very casual place, and might have been named The Malahide Road Majestic. It was like a hotel compared to Kilkenny, and the housemasters were very easy going.

Mountjoy School had started in Mountjoy Square, Dublin, hence its name. Mr Anderson, known as 'the beard' had built up the reputation of the school. It moved to Malahide Road, above Fairview village not long before I arrived in 1951. The school was next door to Clontarf Golf Club and we often collected the golf balls that landed in the school grounds. It was an old red-bricked building that had a new modern building added to it. Here I spent two wasted years studying for a university scholarship.

The teaching at the school was hopeless. I spend two years doing almost nothing, and the only conscientious teacher, Lily Preston, taught French. Willie Le Blanc was housemaster and taught Latin. He was a very poor teacher. Most of the classes were spent discussing the shows and films he had seen at the theatre Royal and other cinemas. The Maths teacher was more like a university lecturer, and was a poor teacher. The science teacher, 'Big Bill' sat at this science desk with a Bunsen burner lighting on either side of him. He seemed more interested in reading the newspaper than in teaching. To relieve the boredom we would blow air into the gas pipes and put out his Bunsen burners. He hardly noticed. At other times we would put golf balls into a glass bowl of acid, put it in a drawer, and the golf balls would hop up and down against the roof of the drawer, he never noticed! I don't think that I ever learnt anything in science class even though I was supposed to be studying for a science entrance scholarship at Trinity College. We could have sat there below the teacher's high bench and read comics for all he cared. The English teacher, Eric Simmons, tried hard and had a dry sense of humour. He would say, 'Do you know the way to Bray, Ruddock?' 'Yes, Sir', 'Hee Haw, you're a silly ass!' You got the impression that the teachers were only putting in time, were completely bored and had been teachers in the one school for far too long. I had a great love of English and history, but I was never encouraged to do an English or history scholarship. No one seemed to give a damn about my educational progress, and I muddled along as best I could. I had got good honours in all my intermediate certificate subjects. I was in an honours class, but I believe the teachers of the pass classes were far superior.

Willie Le Blanc, the housemaster, was a native of Wexford, who took a great interest in hockey. He himself had been a keen hockey player. He was our hockey coach, and prepared us for the senior schools' cup which we won against The King's Hospital. We were not expected to win. I received an inter-provincial trial, but failed to be picked for Leinster.

Wille Le Blanc was an easy going bachelor, and an equally laid back housemaster. Some of us slept in the turret of the old school building, and we never heard the wake up bell. We often missed breakfast, but no one seemed to care.

The sports pitches were not ready, and we were paid money to prepare the soil and sow the grass seed. It was easy to get *exeats* at weekends from the chain-smoking headmaster, William Tate, who was known as 'Tilly'.

I had developed a weak stomach and ulcer as a result of Kilkenny food. The matron at Mountjoy School, Susan Corrigan from Co Carlow, took me under her wing and fed me a special diet in her living room. It was like bed and breakfast in a hotel.

Susan was one of the kindest, most loving, and caring women that I have ever known.

Most Sundays I was invited out to Malahide to the home of Frank and Kit Manning. I came to know them through my brother John, who was then playing the organ in the church at Malahide. Frank Manning was a character who wore black broad brimmed hats and smoked a big pipe. It was he who years earlier arrived at Kilkenny with a monster bag of goodies. Frank was an Englishman who had been traffic manager at Arthur Guinness, but was now retired. Their only child, Gordon, had been lost in the war while flying with the Royal Air Force. They never got over the terrible tragedy. I suppose that I was a kind of substitute son, and they brought me out regularly for Sunday lunch at Portmarnock and Malahide golf clubs. Sometimes Kit would cook at home, and she made a truly delicious trifle. Frank and Kitty were devoted to each other, and they were like the characters in Maupassant's Minuet. I will always treasure their kindness and generosity to me.

The summer between years at Mountjoy School I went to France to visit a penfriend, Jacques Mollay. His father was a cinema manager on the Champs Elyseé, and we got free passes to the films. The Mollays lived in a flat near the Place d'Italie. Jacques brought me on a tour bus to the South of France, down through Dijon, Avignon, and the Mediterranean. It was a fabulous trip. The whole family joined us on the Cote d'Azur for their summer holiday. Jacques was a sissy, a mother's boy, and we did not get on too well. He was to come to Ireland the following year, and I am glad that it did not materialise. The trip gave me a great love of France and all things French. The visit certainly improved my French in sixth form.

The Irish teacher, Mick Franklin, had I think played hurling for Limerick and his idol was Mick Mackey of immortal Limerick teams. We rarely studied Irish, and he was forever telling us a fund of dirty stories. He was more streetwise than the other teachers. Maybe that's because he was a Catholic. He had a fascination with orchitis, which I discovered in later life was inflammation of the testicles. Maybe he suffered from that disease or had prostate problems. Mick knew we were bored with Irish, and he didn't want to bore us anymore.

On Sundays we went to Clontarf parish church which was a twenty-minute walk from the school. It was a traditional conservative congregation and the rector, the Reverend J. B. Neligan, was one of the most boring preachers that I have ever heard. The curate, the Reverend Denholm Moore, was a little more interesting, and he took us for an evening scripture class at school. My path crossed with J. B. Neligan years later as he was pastoral theology lecturer in the divinity school at Trinity College. No one could have made pastoralia so uninteresting. He was simply a dull man.

Miss Harkness' dance academy was in a lane off upper Leeson Street, and we were sent there to learn ballroom dancing. Miss Harkness was a quaint old-fashioned lady who brought girls along as partners from neighbouring schools, such as Margaret's Hall and Diocesan Girls school, both now closed down. The boys lined up on one side of the room and the girls on the other. When we were told to select a partner there was a mad rush to pick the prettiest girl. When the bill for dance lessons appeared on my school bill, the rector of Carlow who paid my fees out of a charity fund, was less than pleased. Was this the best way to use charitable funds? I never did enjoy dancing and the only reason that I went to dances was to pick up a woman.

School dances at various girls' schools were held regularly, and we were invited to Alexandra College, Masonic girls school, Celbridge Collegiate, and Mercers at Castleknock. Alexandra is the only remaining girls school today. These girls boarding schools were full of frustrated young maidens who were always interested in exploratory sex! However dances were heavily supervised, but sometimes we would arrange innocent dates. Testosterone levels were rising, and I began to realise that girls were different from boys.

School dances were held regularly at Mountjoy School. The headmaster, 'Tilly Tate', used to patrol the grounds with a big torch. He was making sure that there was no fornication or copulation behind the bushes. In those days we would not have known what a condom was, and they were certainly not available in holy Catholic Ireland.

'Nuz' Sutton, one of the teachers, ran the tuck shop, and he

was always on duty at school dances. If you ordered pepper-
mints at the counter Nuz would require you to breathe out to
check that you had not been smoking. He was death to smoking.
Nuz also supervised the annual scripture examination, known
as the synod exam. Underneath the desks were hidden Bibles
and Bible aids. Nuz collected a host of Bibles, a veritable mountain and piled them high on a table. He left the assembly hall for
a moment, and when he returned all the books had disappeared.
When he returned Nuz was furious and accused us all of cheat-
ing in a scripture exam.

Leaving Mountjoy was relief and a low-key exit. It was more
like a holiday home than a school. I always regretted that I went
there. It is now a large comprehensive for north Dublin, and one
of its famous pupils is Bono of U2.

CHAPTER 6

The Thank You

Donnelly's old world bar and grocery shop was situated some doors down from our own shop in Tullow Street, Carlow. It was run by Gerald Donnelly and his wife who had spent all their working life in the business. Gerald was a kind gentleman who looked after his customers conscientiously. I don't believe that he ever lost a customer. Most of them came in to the grocery shop for their weekly orders which were written down in their individual passbooks. Credit was given and bills were paid monthly or quarterly. The smell of coffee being ground permeated the shop and the large range of loose biscuits was displayed in an elegant wooden Jacobs display cabinet. Much time was spent in the shop weighing up rice, sago, tapioca, tea and sugar. Nothing was pre-packed in those days. A variety of candles of all shapes and sizes hung from a long iron bar over the long counter. Behind the shop there was a bottling plant where beer was bottled and labelled. At Christmas time a mass of large red candles hung from the ceiling and the counter was laden with boxes of Christmas crackers.

One day when business was quiet, and Gerald was relaxed, he told me the story of how he came by the business. As a teenager Gerald had applied to the previous owner for a job as a messenger boy, which was advertised in the local paper. He did not get the job, but he wrote a letter of thanks to the proprietor for considering him. When the job as messenger boy was next vacant the shop owner remembered Gerald Donnelly's letter of thanks and he wrote and offered him the job. When the owner was retiring from business he offered Gerald the business for a nominal sum. This was all because the owner remembered Gerald's letter of thanks. In an age when people say thanks less often, or seldom write letters of thanks, Gerald's letter written so many years ago speaks volumes.

When I arrived home from my last term at boarding school, Gerald Donnelly had died and his widow was finding it difficult to cope on her own. She kindly offered me a job for the summer and my time was divided between the grocery and the pub. The pub was never very busy, but there were a few regulars who spent the day in the pub, because they had nowhere else to go. They often tried to get drinks on credit and to put it all down on the slate behind the bar. I rarely relented. I had to listen to the same boring stories each day. Fair day was always a busy day in the bar, when farmers did their business in the snug. Sometimes Mrs Donnelly relieved me in the bar, so that I could do work in the bottling plant. The beer arrived from Guinness and Smithwick in big wooden barrels and had to be bottled. First the bottles had to be sterilised, filled with beer, labelled on another machine and corked on another. It was a time-consuming process.

Donnellys, like so many other old shops, is long gone. It was bought by Billy Shaw of 'Shaws Almost Nationwide' and is now a drapery store. I shall always remember that summer that I spent in the grocery and bar trade.

Years later my barman experience came in very useful when I was asked to be barman at a family fiftieth wedding anniversary party at Brittas Bay in Co Wicklow. The guests were naturally elderly and asked for gin and tonic without exception. I did not measure the drinks and dispensed the gin most liberally. They came back for top ups continually, and I was complimented for being such a generous purveyor of gin. Later on in the evening, the hosts asked me to say a few prayers from the wedding service fifty years ago. The guests got a shock when they heard the bar man reciting the prayers. They had no knowledge that I was a clergyman in disguise.

I was accepted for university entrance, but my efforts at achieving a scholarship are best forgotten. That September I was invited to Bishop Foy School in Waterford as a junior master and sports master. I was able to study externally for Trinity College. The school was situated opposite the cathedral, and the back of the building faced on to the Mall. The classrooms are now ESB offices. The school was named after Bishop Nathaniel Foy who was bishop of Waterford in 1691. The present school had been the bishop's palace. The school is long since closed and is now the headquarters of Waterford Corporation.

The headmaster in Waterford was Len Horan who was a perfect gentleman and a great encourager. He had been a good athlete at Trinity, and was still superbly fit. He took an interest in Trinity athletics after graduation, and was always present at the Trinity races as a judge. He looked debonair in morning suit and top hat. He was also a good musician and played the violin with dramatic flair. In ways he was a very lonely man who was married to a very dominant woman. In the background, she fired the cannon balls and ruffled the feathers of some of the staff. I always felt that Len Horan was a man who needed lots of tender loving care.

My duties at Bishop Foy School involved teaching junior French, English and a little Irish. I was nervous taking Irish classes, as the head was an Irish scholar. It was there that I was attracted to a girl for the first time. Carol hailed from Dublin and was one of my pupils. She was a beautiful young woman and I felt that the feelings that I experienced were mutual. I was also given the task of taking Carol for Irish grinds which was unbelievably frustrating. She was pupil and I her teacher, so it remained unrequited love. Her parents were concerned that her studies would suffer and we drifted apart. Carol married a Dublin businessman who died suddenly on holidays, and some years later married again. I hope that she is happy. My wife Jean met Carol when they were both working for an insurance company. I don't know if they exchanged notes. I will probably never meet Carol again in this life, but she taught me tenderness.

Waterford was a sleepy city in the early fifties. The YMCA had a flourishing hockey team as had Waterford City. We played hockey all over the southeast. These were great social occasions and there was much after match drinking. I played hockey for the YMCA and one holiday I returned to play in a cup match. I stayed with one of the players who got quite drunk after the match. My host was asked by a friendly garda to leave his car outside the hotel on the quays and collect it the next day. We walked about three miles to his home and fell into bed.

Our fiercest rivals were the Greenhills hockey team near Wexford. My memories are of a hockey pitch which was ready for silage cutting! There were a number of hurlers on the Greenhills team and they played a robust game – a cross between hockey and hurling. Our big centre forward from Waterford tried to trip up his opposite number, Vin Byrne who didn't take prisoners. Vin Byrne lifted his stick and told our player that if he ever came near him again 'he would cut the balls off him'. That player was afraid to play against Greenhills again. There was one courteous member of the Greenhills team by the name of Nicholas Furlong, now a distinguished journalist and historian. How did they all get round the GAA ban which did not allow them to play foreign games? Greenhills, like so many provincial teams, folded up over the years. While ladies' hockey survives there is virtually no men's hockey in the South East of Ireland.

During the summer months the matron would drive some of the staff out to Dunmore East, where we retired to the local pub by the harbour. None of us had cars. As a student teacher I was paid seventy pounds a year – about ninety euros. I was also provided with free board, lodging and laundry. I was never short or wanted for anything. I was even able to pay university fees out of my salary as well.

The diocese of Waterford had a gentle giant as bishop, Arnold Harvey. He had been a fine sportsman in his youth. He had been an exceptional cricketer at Trinity and had once bowled the immortal W. G. Grace for a 'duck'. Grace came down the wicket and said to Harvey, 'Young man the people came to see me bat, not to see you bowling!' Bishop Harvey lived at Bishopsgrove overlooking the river Suir on the Kilkenny side. On Sundays when he was free he would invite the boy boarders to his home. He would sit in a chair in the garden and teach the boys how to bat and bowl. It was at Bishopsgrove that the bishop showed me his Lambeth chair. At the end of each ten-year Lambeth conference of Anglican bishops a plaque on the back of the chair registered their name. I remember seeing Archbishop McCann of Armagh and Bishop Hodges of Limerick getting off a boat train at Westland Row, carrying their chairs. I presume that the Harvey family still has the chair in their possession.

CHAPTER 7

The Call to Holy Orders

My thoughts were now turning towards ordination. It was no sudden blinding light, but a process which began at confirmation. My mother was a very committed churchwoman, and her commitment rubbed off on me. Confirmation in Saint Canice's Cathedral, Kilkenny was a moving experience for me. Precentor Jack Nelson was a kind of godfather and his influence of simple, saintly piety left a great impression on me as a young man. He was also a quiet emotional preacher who took his themes from life. He was in and out of our shop and home regularly.

This is in marked contrast to clergy today who in the main have given up on visiting. Nothing is more rewarding and satisfying than visiting people in their homes. I remember a Roman Catholic in Wexford married to a Church of Ireland lady. He told me that I was the first priest to visit his home and he deeply appreciated my visit. On another occasion on my first visit to a farmer's house as rector, he said that this was a very special occasion. He took down a bottle of brandy and we celebrated that simple visit. I enjoyed many more visits to that couple's home. On another occasion I happened to visit a home when the wife was about to stab her husband with a kitchen knife.

The clergy of my youth contributed to my desire to be ordained. The ministry also offered me the opportunity to mix with people and help the needy. Dean George Seaver also influenced me to be ordained. His sermons moved me greatly. Here was a man who could have spent his life in the academic world but chose to be a parish clergyman. I only met him once afterwards in a Donegal hotel where he was enjoying a glass of Guinness.

When I told Bishop Harvey that I was contemplating holy orders he said that he would support my application for the divinity school at Trinity. There were grants to help students with student fees and accommodation expenses. Bishop Harvey was chairman of the grants committee and I got a generous annual grant. He was one of the kindest men that I have ever met. Years later I was invited back to preach in Waterford Cathedral at a Bishop Foy School service and I thought of Bishop Arnold Harvey who opened doors for me.

His wife was a different kettle of fish. Mrs Harvey was a very dominant lady indeed and sat on the school board of governors. She was in and out of the school monotonously and checked up on everything. I am sure that she was a thorn in the flesh for the headmaster, but he endured it all.

I was accepted for training in the divinity school. Life at Bishop Foy School ended with the school dance, and on the next day I travelled to Dublin on a railway that is no more. There was a train from Waterford to Macmine Junction, a few miles north of Wexford. Here I changed trains to take the Wexford-Dublin train.

In Dublin there was a hostel for us at 25 and 26 Mountjoy Square. Each day we walked down to Trinity to attend lectures. We were given a five pence ticket for the university buffet and it would buy a bowl of soup and a cup of tea. As we walked to college one of our pastimes was to mark the passing women out of ten! Coming home in the evening we were sometimes approached by the 'ladies of the night' in Upper Gardiner Street.

The warden of the hostel was the Reverend Michael Ferrar and he was a celibate. He was known as the 'bagman' because he carried a Gladstone bag to college. He was a very austere, bureaucratic man who ruled with a rod of iron. When we got colds we were put to bed with weak tea. Ferrar believed in starving a cold. Lying in bed we were ravenous and fellow students were dispatched to Mooney's pub to bring back ham sandwiches and large bottles of Guinness.

Next door to the divinity hostel there was a Catholic club. Ferrar arranged a table tennis match, and he was very excited at this ecumenical outreach. We won the match, and I got brownie points. There were nights when we arrived back at the hostel worse for wear, and I can remember one night when I fell asleep inside the main door. Some of my friends put me to bed. It is ironic that wine importers now own the buildings and it is stocked with champagne.

Each of us had to read evening prayer or compline on a rota. The warden prepared us for these services. Sometimes the assistant warden, Allen Wilson, took us, but he did not keep us long. On one occasion the warden noticed that I was dressed up for some outing. I was being prepared for my turn to read the service. He went on and on and the name of the game was to keep me late. My temper was rising and suddenly I picked up a prayer book and flung it at him. 'Go and practice what you preach' I shouted and stormed out. I knew that I would receive an eviction notice and shortly afterwards my residence was terminated.

Sometimes the warden would have visitors to come and speak to us. He invited the former Archbishop of Dublin Dr Arthur Barton to speak to us. He was a fine communicator and superb preacher. After his talk there was a time for questions. He was tackled about his membership of the Masonic order because he was a staunch mason. He tried to move on to other questions but the questioner persisted – can a Christian be a member of a pre-Christian society? Bishop Barton almost exploded, and became very angry. A raw nerve had been touched. I was disappointed that he could not discuss the issue logically with us. The meeting ended poorly, and the bishop did not come out of the session with flying colours.

Visitors stayed in 'the prophets' chamber, and two prominent Unionist Clergy, one from Northern Ireland, came to stay. Late one night, led by Walton Empey, later to become Archbishop of Dublin we marched up the stairs to the prophets' chamber singing *Kevin Barry*. Outside the Unionists' room we ceremoniously burned the Union Jack.

One student, Donald Atkinson who was a heavy sleeper failed to turn up to read Morning Prayer. I put together at the time a poem to mark the occasion to the tune of *Kevin Barry*:

In Mountjoy Square one Sunday morning
    at the break of early day
Donald Atkinson slept, sweetly sleeping
    and his thoughts were far away.
Come down you lazy fellow
    'the bag' was heard to say,
Donald Atkinson slept sweetly sleeping
    and his thoughts were far away.

As expected I was evicted as being a troublesome rebel, but some weeks later I got a job in Wesley College on Saint Stephen's Green as an assistant housemaster. In return for taking prep and helping with games I received free board and lodging. The principal, the Reverend Gerald Myles, was a strict Methodist who ran a tight ship. Chapel was compulsory on Sunday evenings at 5.00 pm. Gerry Myles preached every Sunday and we listened as he told us how he won the war in the Royal Air Force.

During term time I had various part time jobs to make ends meet. One job took me to a prep school in Rathgar, called Glenart School. It was run by a Doctor Charles Bowlby who had a patch over one eye. I don't know whether Bowlby was a doctor, but there was something very shifty about him. When he exhausted his credit on the south side of Dublin he headed for Howth on the north side. I was never paid for the hours that I spent coaching soccer, and I was one of the many creditors of the infamous Charles Bowlby.

Another job that I had involved taking a young boy for grinds. He was a difficult boy who found it hard to communicate. He was the grandson of a Church of Ireland bishop. Strangely enough neither of the parents spoke to me when I visited their house. The father went out of his way to avoid me and there seemed to be a lot of tension in the home. The boy's sister had an unhappy marriage and left her husband. At her wedding her grandfather bishop turned to the groom and said, 'She is precious to me. Will you look after her well?' That was not to be.

I was also asked to teach in Bagnalstown national school for a few months. As a result of this work I was asked to hold the fort in Fethard-on Sea School in south Co Wexford. This was one of the most exciting experiences of my young life and landed me in the midst of a controversy that became a national news item for many months.

CHAPTER 8

'Scabs, Beware of the lead in the boycott village'

Life in Ireland in the 1950s was predictable and uneventful. Ecumenism was almost unknown and there was little or no social or religious interaction among different denominations. The Roman Catholic Church exercised great power in the community and country and there seemed little hope of any change. Archbishop McQuaid in Dublin and Bishop Browne in Galway ruled with rods of iron. The bishops' lenten pastorals were full of instructions to uphold the Catholic faith and to avoid 'mixed marriages'.

There was a ban on Catholics attending 'the Protestant' Trinity College, though some ignored the ban. Contraception was one of the greatest evils of all, as it might decrease the Catholic population. Meat was banned on Fridays. Bishop Keogh of Kildare and Leighlin always wrote deeply spiritual lenten pastorals.

It was in the County of Wexford and the Diocese of Ferns that a dramatic event took place in 1957 which challenged the power of the Catholic Church, and the rights of individual freedom. The conservative Bishop Stuanton was the Catholic Bishop of Ferns. When a Protestant builder arrived to do work at the Bishop's house, the Bishop put out his hand for the builder to kiss his ring. The builder, very much an anti-Romanist, refused to do obeisance to the bishop. He did not kiss the bishop's ring. It was all part of the power game.

Rumours began to trickle through the countryside that there were strange goings on in south Wexford in Fethard-On-Sea. There was talk of intimidation of Protestants but there was little concrete evidence about what was going on. There was talk of a boycott which reminded people of the sinister boycotts of the 19th century. Fethard-On-Sea began to appear in the news media. To describe it as being on the sea was a misnomer as it was situated two miles from the nearest beach, and some fifteen miles south of the seaport of New Ross. Fethard was a sleepy hamlet visited in the summer by a small number of holiday makers who had houses and mobile homes there.

To understand the Fethard boycott one has to look at the Tilson case in Oldcastle, County Meath. It was a watershed in civil and ecclesiastical law in Ireland. When I was rector of Oldcastle, Miss Mitty Tilson, the last surviving member of the family told me the story. Her brother worked in Dublin Corporation and married a Roman Catholic. In 1950 the marriage broke up and Ernest Tilson brought the children to Oldcastle. After some weeks the boys were put in the Bird's Nest, a Protestant home in Dún Laoire. The *Evening Herald* announced that Mrs Tilson was taking legal action to have the *Ne Temere* decree enforced and the children brought up as Catholics.

In court Judge Gavin Duffy was 'Spitting fire', and one commentator alleged, Duffy was a 'prosecuting judge'. The highest court in the land upheld the decree of the Roman Church on the basis of Article 44 of the Irish Constitution. This judgement appeared to endorse the phrase 'Home Rule is Rome Rule'. The eloquent and French-sounding Seán McBride SC was Minister for Foreign Affairs in the then inter-party government. He was sometimes referred to as the voice of the new Ireland and a champion of the liberal point of view. Along with Dr Noel Browne, McBride had founded Clann Na Poblacha, a new party which would challenge the establishment. With Fine Gael they were able to form a government in opposition to Fianna Fáil. Dr Noel Browne got little or no support from this alliance for his Mother and Child Scheme. Here again the conservative Catholic Taoiseach, John A. Costello, bowed to pressure from the Catholic hierarchy and the health scheme was shelved.

Seán McBride had spoken at a Jewish discussion group of the rights of minorities. Ernie Tilson's mother wrote to McBride about her son's case, but he never replied. So much for the rights of minorities.

Mitty Tilson alleged that her family had been boycotted in Oldcastle and verbally abused in the streets. Her dress making business dried up. Her rector could not cope with the situation and wanted it all to go away. However her local Catholic doctor continued to give her business. Mitty was afraid to go out to church as she would meet Catholic antagonists coming out of Mass on the way home. Years later I attended the funeral of Ernie Tilson in Shanganagh cemetery near Bray in Co Wicklow. The legal judgement in the Tilson case spawned Fethard in Co Wexford. The judgement was based on the special place of the Roman Catholic Church in the state.

'You may or you Maynooth'

The *Ne Temere* decree of 1908 stated that in the event of a 'mixed marriage' the Protestant partner had to sign a document agreeing to bring up any children of the marriage as Roman Catholics. This was simply church law and not civil law. Article 44 of the Constitution stated that 'the State recognises the special position of the Holy Catholic Apostolic and Roman Church as the guardian of the faith professed by the great majority of the people". This Constitution was put together by Éamon De Valera, an ardent conservative and devoted Catholic. The county councillors of Westmeath called for the amendment of Article 44. Thankfully that good and liberal Taoiseach, Jack Lynch, spearheaded the Referendum that abolished this sectarian law.

Prior to 1908 it was common practice for partners to make no promises to any church and, if children were born, the boys would go to the church of the father and the girls would follow the mother. *Matrimonia Mixta* issued by that good Pope Paul VI in 1970 repealed all previous regulations and as a result of it the non Roman Catholic partner in a mixed marriage was no longer required to make any promises.

The Fethard-On-Sea boycott seemed to drag us back to more bitter times. Sheila Cloney was married to a strong farmer, Sean Cloney of Dungulph Castle. Sheila, a member of the Church of Ireland, had signed the piece of paper to bring up her children as Catholics. When her daughter Eileen reached school-going age, Sheila had qualms of conscience. She wanted her daughter to attend the Church of Ireland School and not the Catholic school. The local Catholic curate, Fr Stafford, demanded that the child attend the Catholic school. He was persistent.

On 27 April 1957 Sheila took the car and travelled to Wexford with her daughters. Here she abandoned the car and travelled on to Belfast. Here she seems to have been in contact with two very right wing Unionist politicians, Desmond Boal QC and Norman Porter MP.

Three days after Sheila Cloney's disappearance a barrister arrived at Sean Cloney's home with 'terms of settlement'. Sean was to sell Dungulph Castle and they were to emigrate to Canada or Australia. Here the children would be brought up as Protestants. The story spread rapidly and a reporter arrived at Dungulph. Sean Cloney told the reporter that once Sheila gets an idea in her head a regiment of solders wouldn't change her. A former rector said that Sheila was no one's fool. From Belfast she travelled with her daughters to Scotland where her husband Sean visited her. This was all well documented in the movie of the saga, *A Love Divided*. Sean and Sheila's clash of interests and preference led to one God-awful domestic row. Sheila and Sean fought over flies going up walls for years afterwards.

The local Church of Ireland people were blamed for enticing Sheila away from her home. They were also accused of giving Sheila money to travel. Father Stafford, the curate at nearby Poulfur, decided to declare open war. The Kilkenny liberal writer, Hubert Butler wrote 'There was a thunderous pronouncement from the altar of Poulfur Chapel'. I got the distinct impression that the Roman Catholic curate, a strong well-built man, was given to outbursts of righteous and indeed unrighteous rages. Otherwise he was quite humane.

War declared from Poulfur pulpit caused a boycott of all the Church of Ireland parishioners in the village. The local general merchant, Leslie Gardiner, saw his business dry up as did the local newsagent, Betty Cooper. Miss Knipe, the piano teacher, lost eleven of the twelve pupils. People stopped buying milk from the Protestant farmers. The Catholic teacher in the Church of Ireland School also left and the school had to close temporarily.

There were continual denials of a boycott in Fethard-On-Sea but one Sunday morning an *Irish Times* reporter was present at Mass. He heard the priest say, 'the boycott will continue'. This was front-page news on *The Irish Times* next morning, and the boycott was receiving national interest. In the summer of 1957 in the Church of the Immaculate Conception, Wexford and in the presence of the Archbishops of Armagh and Dublin, the Bishop of Galway preached the homily at the Catholic Truth Society Mass. Browne defended the boycott and called it a 'peaceful protest'. The boycott was a response to a 'concerted campaign to entice or kidnap Catholic children and deprive them of their faith', he said. Paddy Kilroy SC was the legal adviser to Bishop Browne of Galway. Browne ignored Kilroy's explicit instructions to 'cool Fethard' and he resigned as Browne's legal adviser. Paddy Kilroy was horrified at Browne's intransient stance.

A promise is a promise

Hubert Butler of Kilkenny, at a lecture that he gave in Dublin, was very critical of the Roman Catholic Church. The Papal Nuncio walked out. Butler had little love for Rome and took a personal interest in the Fethard boycott. Butler wished to encourage people from all over the southeast to buy goods from the boycotted shopkeepers. The local Church of Ireland Bishop, Dr Percy Phair, saw this move as 'senseless provocation'. The bishop's stance was one of appeasement. He was an old man who was totally out of his depth in this situation. He may have worked behind the scenes, but it was not evident. Butler, the liberal and Phair, the conservative were poles apart.

A Deafening Silence

The Church of Ireland bishops hid their heads in the sand and said nothing. This was in sharp contrast to Archbishop J. A. F. Gregg of Armagh who years before denied the validity of a promise exerted under pressure. When the controversy surfaced years later a writer stated: 'Protestants in their spinelessness had left the defence of their liberties to liberal Catholics like Dr Noel Browne and humanists like Dr Owen Skeffington of Trinity College.'

Of the Ne Temere decree Archbishop Gregg had once written: 'The decree could be withdrawn at any time or thrust into the capacious wastepaper basket kept in Rome for the reception of papal utterances that have miscarried.' In 1983 the Ne Temere decree was set aside and oral promises substituted. For the first time the rights of both parties to a marriage were recognised. Years later I was asked to baptise a baby in the Church of Ireland tradition. The marriage had taken place in a Roman Catholic

Church. I immediately rang the kind Bishop of Ferns, Dr Donal Herlihy and asked him if he had any objection. 'You do Norman what you think in conscience you should do.' I baptised the baby in the presence of a Catholic priest friend. The baby was baptised in both traditions and I'm sure there was joy in heaven.

Fethard-On-Sea became a curiosity as people came from far and near to see this phenomenon of a boycott village. *Time*, *Life* and other international journalists arrived to cover the story. Hubert Butler wrote in *Escape from the Anthill* that 'it was a collision between human nature and the immutable principles of the Roman Catholic Church.' An eminent barrister, Donal Barrington wrote that 'the boycott is the most terrible thing that has happened in this part of the country since the civil war'.

A Norman is Coming

Between terms at Trinity I had been doing supply teaching in primary schools. Out of the blue the bishop, Dr Phair asked me if I would re-open the school in Fethard-On-Sea and teach there right through the summer holidays. The children had lost a good few school days. I had never heard of Fethard but the challenge of the boycott excited me. My journey there began one Sunday evening after a choral festival in the cathedral at Old Leighlin and tea at the old deanery. I was driven to Fethard by a very nervous clergyman, the Reverend Talbot, rector of Bannow. It seemed a long journey in his little car and there was very little communication as he drove along. Talbot never mentioned the boycott, and I thought this strange as he lived in the next parish. I was frightened. Was I a fool to come to this divided community? It was late when we reached Leslie and Pearl Gardiner's house. They had kindly offered me board and lodging.

On Monday morning faces peered from behind the curtains. No one spoke to me. I now understand what 'being sent to Coventry' was all about. A notice was pinned to the school door: 'Scabs, beware of the lead in the boycott village.'

I handed the sign to the Garda, but I was nervous. There had been rifle fire on several nights outside Protestant homes. When I phoned my mother she advised me to come home. I was determined to challenge this boycott even though I was seen as a scab.

There were about fifteen children of all ages in the school who were mostly from farming families. They were lovely children and were totally confused with what was going on. It was essential that their school life should be normal and that I set out to do. We spent much of the time playing games and having fun. Some forty years later I met one of those pupils when I was doing my chaplain's rounds in hospital. Ecumenical relations had changed out of all recognition over that generation.

One day a school inspector arrived and he carried out a very hostile examination of my timetable. He was a bitter pill indeed. Most of the children came to school by state transport and the inspector proceeded to drive out the country to check mileages from the school to children's homes. Each child at that time who lived three and a half miles from the school was entitled to free transport. The inspector arrived back from his mileage check. He was in foul humour and insinuated that the distances were wrong. He then examined the children in a very aggressive manner. It was like an inquisition. I have always regretted that I did not complain to the Department of Education about the inspector's behaviour. I could see where his sympathy and loyalty lay.

For me the summer of 1957 was an idyllic time. It was a lovely summer and I had good digs at Leslie and Pearl Gardiner's home. Their home was over the shop and almost opposite the school. During the summer holidays when the Gardiner children were home from boarding school at Bishop Foy's School Waterford they were great company. We played tennis on the village court and swam in Baginbun beach and Grange. In the evenings Leslie Gardiner and myself played endless games of draughts. This was long before the days of TV. Our summer social life made us forget the boycott which was festering in the background. One of the most exciting events of that summer was the day that a large number of whales were washed up on Grange beach. The whales were marooned in the shallows. There was no way to get them back in deep water again. The whales died and lorries took them off to a bone meal factory.

The Reverend Adrian Fisher was a local rector, friendly but eccentric. One Sunday he preached on the importance of saints and encouraged us all to come to church on Saint James's day during the following week. We arrived for the Communion service, but the rector totally forgot about it! During the worst days of the boycott I never heard Adrian Fisher say an unkind word. Some years later he enlisted as a chaplain in the British Army.

To give parishioners a lift we organised a social dance in the school. It was a great success, and the people came from far and near to support the event. One of the most moving events that summer was being called out early one morning to the little harbour. An ailing fisherman had died as he steered his fishing boat into Fethard harbour. The scene reminded me of the words of the psalmist – 'and he brought them to the haven they longed for.' There in the boat I prayed over the fisherman. That fisherman loved the sea, and it was a coming home as his boat drifted into the safety of the harbour. He was laid out in the shed behind Gardiner's shop.

The Clouds Lift
The late Dr Noel Browne raised the boycott issue in the Dáil. Browne was always the champion of the underdog. The late Brendan Corish, TD for Wexford, questioned the Taoiseach (the prime minister) whether there was a boycott. Could anyone be more naïve? Several deputies in the house shouted 'nonsense'. The Taoiseach, Dr Éamon De Valera called it 'ill conceived and futile'. It didn't lose De Valera any votes. The Fethard-On-Sea boycott was an embarrassment. The papal nuncio summoned Bishop Staunton of Ferns to the nunciature in Dublin to have the boycott called off immediately. The communists were persecuting Roman Catholics in Hungary and it would not be seemly for Catholics to be intimidating Protestants in Ireland. Father Stafford received the news with a heavy heart, and it must have taken great courage for him to accept the word from Rome. Give the man his due, he went into Betty Cooper's shop and bought a packet of cigarettes. That was a powerful symbolic act.

An Affair of the Heart
The whole saga had a sequel in Rowe Street Church in Wexford on Pentecost Sunday 1998. On that day we had a memorable and moving service to mark the bi-centenary of the 1798 rebellion. Both bishops of Ferns were present as well as Mary McAleese,

President of Ireland. This was one of the finest acts of worship that I had ever attended. It was planned by an imaginative, ecumenical committee under Jim Fegan, administrator of Wexford parish.

Bishop Comiskey gave the homily that day, but he focused on the Fethard-On-Sea boycott rather than 1798. Was the burning of Scullabogue barn of lesser importance? No one had been killed in Fethard, as opposed to the great loss of life in 1798. Some people were very upset when Fethard became the centrefold of the homily. Be that as it may, Bishop Brendan seized the moment, and asked the Church of Ireland to accept his apologies for the boycott. He then embraced the Church of Ireland Bishop to sustained applause from the overflow congregation. Seated there, were 1798 senators from all over the world, including Jim Bolger, former prime minister of New Zealand. Writing in *The Irish Times* at a later date, Bishop Comiskey wrote that 'apologies were due for a time when blind intolerance ruled. When one loves another it is not at all hard to ask forgiveness.' Bishop Brendan further wrote 'for me personally ecumenism has moved from a subject to be studied to an affair of the heart.' When the late Sean Cloney and his wife Sheila heard the news of Pentecost 1998 it must have warmed their hearts. While some people objected to the way that Bishop Brendan had changed the agenda in Rowe Street Church that day, it was still a courageous act. It received great publicity. It is my prayer that the late Bishop Browne of Galway and the late Father William Stafford have seen the new ecumenical light burning brightly in Co Wexford.

How could it all have happened?
The Fethard-On-Sea boycott is an enigma. Sheila Cloney and her daughters returned home again and normal life continued. The children were educated at home. Billy Colfer, in *The Hook Peninsula*, wrote that 'the shocking nature of the boycott possibly motivated the improved interdenominational links which developed in Fethard in later years.' The Reverend Jimmy Grant later became rector of Fethard. A friend told me 'that the most popular Jimmy Grant restored light, fun and wonderful neighbourliness to the whole Hook peninsula'. Jimmy Grant was later

the victim of poor health and had to take early retirement. He was my classmate.

Would the boycott have taken place if a less emotional priest was resident there? I do not know, though the Hook area had a history of historical bitterness ever since the Earls of Ely came there. A commentator on the times said, 'Father Stafford was a hot headed bully. He and the old parish priest, Father Allen went over the head of Monsignor Hickey of New Ross to try to conjure support for the boycott from Bishop Staunton of Ferns.' It was Stafford who had first used the word 'boycott' at Mass. In the light of inter-church relations in Co Wexford today, the boycott seems like a fairytale. Today we have interchurch baptisms, weddings and funerals in each others churches. The Roman Catholic clergy in Ferns are the warmest group of men in the world. One other present day phenomenon in Ferns diocese is that of the nine Church of Ireland rectors, four were brought up in the Catholic Church. Three of them were Catholic priests. This cross fertilisation is a healthy sign and when Rome recognises Anglican orders, there is nothing to stop us all being one. A comical priest said that when all the Church Of Ireland clergy are ex-Catholics, it will be simple to turn the sign around.

One of Father William Stafford's successors, Joe McGrath, exercised a loving pastoral ministry on the Hook to all creeds and none. Father Joe was present in the Church Of Ireland church when I preached at a harvest some years ago. When Sheila Cloney's daughter died, her funeral took place in both churches, in one church on one evening and in the other on the following day. This was a fitting epitaph, a closing scene, and light years away from the feelings of 1957.

CHAPTER 9

And so he rose and twitched his mantle blue
Tomorrow to fresh woods and pastures new
Longfellow

When Father William Stafford went in to the Protestant shop to buy cigarettes it was a visible sign of the end of the boycott. When I left Fethard-On-Sea in October 1957 to return to university, the village had almost returned to normality. One of the most helpful fruits of the boycott was the collection that the shipyard workers in Belfast made for the Fethard shopkeepers. The monies had been sent to the local rector to distribute. I received a generous cheque for my services in the school and it kept me in pocket money all winter. On top of that I had been paid by the Department of Education as a temporary untrained teacher. I was sad leaving Fethard after the excitement of the previous months and I knew that I would never again experience such an event.

Once again I was back in the Divinity School to finish my final year. The warden of the residential hostel, Michael Ferrar had invited me to become a resident again. I think he missed the excitement of my presence and he needed a good table tennis player for the hostel team. It was a pretty easy regime and the only major requirement was attendance at chapel on Friday nights.

We were high-spirited students and always playing tricks on each other. On one occasion we hid up the stairs from the public phone and had an innocent student paged to take a call. Our accomplice on the other end of the phone pretended to be the archbishop. The 'archbishop' asked the innocent one to kneel on the stone floor for a blessing. This he proceeded to do and he was told that he would receive special merit for kneeling on the cold stone floor.

With arts degrees under our belt we settled down to study for the divinity testimonium. This was the academic requirement for ordination and included Greek. I was never a Greek scholar and we were required to attend elementary Greek lectures. These lectures were given by the austere Professor W. B.

Stanford. The lectures were held at 9.00 am and at 9.00 am exactly Stanford locked the door. No latecomers were admitted. We were treated like schoolboys and anyone who laughed was quickly evicted. On one occasion someone let an alarm clock ring, and he was immediately suspended.

Romances began to blossom, though prospective rectors preferred new curates to be single. One northern bishop did not allow curates to marry for three years. He would ask would-be ordinands at interview if they were married or engaged. 'No, my lord.' 'Then stay that way,' the bishop replied.

At a school dance at Wesley College I met a beautiful Jewish girl. She was from a very orthodox family who were strict about religious observance. She was one of the first real loves of my life. I never did confide to her that I was studying for the Christian ministry and she got a shock when one of my friends told her. When I left Amiens Street station, Dublin, to be ordained in Belfast she came to see me off. I only saw her once afterwards when we passed each other on a Dublin Street.

God's Army
The divinity school in Trinity College was a very traditional institution. Sadly it was replaced by a theological college at Rathgar, which lessened the ties with the university. The gentle Professor J. E. L. Oulton, known as 'Gerry', was the religious professor of divinity and he took the senior year lectures. Dr Oulton died in my junior year and he was replaced by his assistant, Dr R. Hartford, the Archbishop King's Professor of Divinity. This meant that I had Hartford for junior and senior years. R. R. Hartford was known as 'Dicky' and he married Diana, the Bishop of Kilmore's daughter. He was very ambitious and some asked if the archbishop did not have a daughter.

One day I met Professor Hartford in College Park as he watched a rugby match. The bishopric of Ossory was vacant and Hartford was a native of the diocese. He was always keen to be Bishop of Ossory. Hartford asked me whose names were being considered. Listing a few, I told him that I believed his own name was in the hat. 'Have a *Craven A* (a cigarette), Ruddock, and come for tea.' R. R. was a friendly man and if we fared badly in an exam and needed a few extra marks he would intercede for us. He would have a quiet word with the examiners. He also got us valuable bursaries from college trusts. Once a year he invited us to his house for tea.

In those days Professor Hartford was responsible for placing students in curacies. He tried to get me to go to Ballymena where my brother had been curate. He also suggested Cavan town. I did not feel that I would get along with the rector of Ballymena and Cavan seemed like the backwoods. He became exasperated with me and said, 'Ruddock, you get completely under my skin.' I replied that the feeling was mutual! Eventually I agreed to go to Saint Stephen's parish off the Shankill Road, Belfast. The rector there was a friendly southerner, J. R. Musgrave who had been at school with my brothers at the King's Hospital school.

As students we were assigned as lay readers to Dublin parishes. I was sent to Saint Mark's Church in Pearse Street where Canon George Hobson was rector. This church is now a centre of the Assemblies Of God church. One evening as we processed into church Hobson asked me who was preaching tonight. He assessed the number of people in church by counting the coins. The waitresses in Trinity attended St Mark's and one Monday morning one of them asked me where I had dug up the sermon.

I had preached the sermon the previous day, and I thought that I had not done badly. The Trinity waitress brought me down to earth. Some years later a Dublin rector was looking for a locum and approached Archbishop Caird for help. 'How about Canon Hobson,' the Archbishop suggested. 'But, your grace, he died a few years ago,' the rector replied. 'Well if you manage to get him you will fill your church.'

On another occasion we attended Saint Augustine's Church to support one of our student colleagues who was assisting at the service. St Augustine's was adjacent to Mountjoy Prison, but is long since demolished. The visiting preacher spoke about Africa and he told us that there were ghosts behind every tree. We were splitting ourselves laughing. He then spoke about the tigers in Africa! There are no tigers on that continent.

It was at this time that I came to know the Reverend Noel Willoughby. He was on holidays and came to see a game of cricket in Carlow. We were a player short and we roped Noel to play. He came in at number eleven and managed to block the ball until the runs were hit off by the other batsman. When he became a bishop in later life he said that bishops were good blockers! Noel invited me out to Bray where he was a curate. The rector there, Canon Ernest Campbell, told us the amusing story of his days as curate at Saint George's Church, Dublin. There were daily services there, and few if any parishioners turned up. The treasurer was concerned about the electricity costs. 'The angels and archangels are worshipping here with us,' Campbell stated. 'Yes,' said the treasurer, 'but they are not paying for the electricity!'

June 1958 arrived and I had completed divinity testimonium successfully. It was a miracle that I scraped though Greek. I climbed on to the Enterprise train at Amiens Street, Dublin and I was on my way to a pre-ordination retreat at Murlough House in Co Down. There was great excitement on the train that day because the film actor Cary Grant was on board. He was on his way to a film premiere in Belfast. He was an extremely good-looking man who had several minders.

CHAPTER 10

The Home of King Billy

My knowledge of the North of Ireland was minimal. As a boy I was invited to stay with relatives in Bessbrook, near Newry. I enjoyed these holidays. One of the highlights was travelling on the narrow gauge tram from Bessbrook to Newry. It passed under the great viaduct of the Dublin-Belfast railway. Sometimes the carriages derailed and we had to lift the carriages on to the track again. The narrow gauge railway is no more. It is sad because it would have been a great tourist attraction. I also attended orange processions and attended the black preceptory sham fight at Scarva, Co Down. Here King Billy always defeated King James!

My only other incursion into the North was to see Ireland play France at rugby at Ravenhill, Belfast. Ireland won and I still remember Jack Kyle's drop goal from half way. He was one of the most exciting footballers that I have ever seen.

In July 1958 I was made a deacon at Saint Anne's Cathedral, Belfast with six others. We seven were gathered together at the vestry door, and the dean whisked past us without a word of welcome. What an introduction to ministry. Immediately after the ordination I took the Liverpool boat with my mother and we travelled down to Farnham in Surrey to stay with my mother's sister, Ada. Ada was a wonderful person and a great hostess. It was a lovely holiday in preparation for ministry in Belfast.

My first assignment in Saint Stephen's parish was to travel with the scouts who were camping in the glens of Antrim at Cushendall. It was a painful experience for me, as the scoutmaster could not keep control. It was chaotic. It was nationalist countryside, and one night the Union Jack was stolen from the flagpole. I was staying at the Trinity College Mission on the Crumlin Road and not far from the prison. Here eight to ten single curates lived and the mission was run by a warden who looked after the church nearby. We paid a monthly rent which helped to subsidise the mission. The warden expected us to take part in the services at the mission, but we were already stretched in our own parishes. We were also busy in the evenings. The warden brought in stringent rules and expected us to be present at early morning worship. The cook was instructed not to serve breakfast after nine am. These draconian rules annoyed us and one night unannounced five of us left for two flats. The cook, Winnie Whinton resigned in sympathy and she became our housekeeper and cook. The Reverends Ian Patterson and Jim Moore lived in one flat and Donald Atkinson, my brother Charlie and myself lived in another along the Antrim road.

All hell broke loose next morning when our exodus was discovered. The Bishop, Cyril Elliott, was furious and believed that 'the recalcitrant Ruddocks' were behind it all. The mission took a severe dip in income. News of the rebel clergy spread far and wide. The following year Donald Atkinson and myself moved into digs with Winnie Whinton at Silverstream Parade in north Belfast. We were treated like lords and had the run of her house. Winnie, an ardent unionist, had been married to a Kerryman, and was now a widow. She was one of the kindest women that I have ever known, and she had a great sense of humour. She would knock on our bedroom doors in the morning and ask us what we would like for breakfast. It was heaven compared to the mission house.

Saint Stephen's parish of eight hundred families lay between the Falls and Shankill Roads. Many of the people who attended the church came in from the suburbs. Daughters came in daily to visit their 'mammies' who babysat for them. When the new motorway was built through the parish, it decimated the houses and the parish was amalgamated with Saint Luke's further up the Shankill Road. Jimmy Musgrave was the rector, a southerner and not unlike Frank Sinatra in appearance. He was a very typical cleric of his generation and ran the parish on traditional lines. He was a friendly man who was encouraging and always treated me as a colleague.

Each parish organisation had its annual outing, which were generally all day affairs. The curate was expected to travel on the bus and be a kind of Billy Butlin's redcoat. I was expected to be comedian and singer all the way home. I didn't enjoy these outings very much.

The parishioners were loyalists to the core. Most of the men were members of the Canon Irvine Memorial Orange Lodge. It had been founded by the first rector. Coming from the south I was looked on as a Fenian. While some of the Orangemen were good churchmen, most of them only turned up for the annual Orange Lodge service. I found this hypocritical and asked the rector to be excused. Word reached the bishop who summoned me to bishop's house. Bishop Elliott was a staunch Orangeman and walked in the orange procession every twelfth of July. He looked on me as a rebel as I was one of the curates who walked out of the mission house the previous year. Bishop Elliott told me in no uncertain terms that if I wished to stay in Northern Ireland I would have to stop reading *The Irish Times* and start reading the *Belfast Telegraph*. Ironically that paper is now owned by the southern newspaper baron, Sir Anthony O'Reilly.

Bishop Elliott was an old fashioned man. He was a bachelor and one of the last bishops to wear gaiters. He had a squeaky feminine voice and was not the world's greatest orator. He was, however, a fund of amusing stories. When he was a rector in the shipyard area of Belfast, a beggar came to his door. The beggar took up some grass and began to eat it to show how hungry he was. 'Go round the back,' the Bishop said, 'The grass is longer!'

I was also depressed and ill in Belfast, spending time in the City Hospital. Excessive vomiting had damaged my balance nerve and for some time I needed a walking stick. For some reason I was sent to Purdysburn Hospital for electric shock treatment which terrified me. I was reminded of Mac Murphy in *One flew over the cuckoo's nest*.

My mother travelled all the way from home in Carlow to visit me and she was visibly upset when she saw me in hospital. She brought with her a lovely bunch of sweet smelling red roses. Since then I have always loved red roses. My mother was never a demonstrative or emotional woman but the tears flowed as she hugged me. I have never felt so close to my mother. As Jesus said of Mary who washed his feet, 'It is a lovely thing that she has done to me.' My illness was probably brought on by a hectic social life. To escape the drabness of Belfast life I socialised with a young lady in the choir. It was company I longed for, as I was lonely. Edith, my girlfriend, introduced me to her friends and she was my only sanity.

Polarisation was brought home to me during World Refugee year. When the collection was complete, a woman, a pillar of the church, handed me the cheque. 'Make sure no Catholics get any of this money,' she said. 'If a man fell off a ladder would you ask him his religion before you picked him up?' I replied. That made her think.

My rector did not feel that I was cut out to live in the Unionist culture and he advised me to look for an opening in the South. Luckily that same month there was an advertisement for a curate in Christ Church, Leeson Park. I went down to Dublin for an interview, and the rector Victor Dungan offered me the curacy. I was delighted. On the 31 August 1960 I packed all my belongings into my Morris Minor and headed south for Dublin. I felt a great sense of freedom as I headed for the border. I thought of Charles Wesley's hymn:

My chains fell off, my heart was free;
I rose, went forth, and followed thee.

CHAPTER 11

The Gay Bachelor

When I arrived in Dublin I lived in a comfortable bed-sit in Lower Leeson Street, before it became a haven for fashionable nightclubs. I didn't realise how vulnerable I was as a single man until the events of one Saturday evening. Late in the evening the bell rang and a parishioner, John, arrived at my door. He had always been very warm and encouraging to me since I arrived in the parish, and I enjoyed his company. Inside in my flat he proceeded to tell me that he was gay and that he was in love with me. I was scared stiff – John was a big man – what was I going to do? The situation needed careful handling, and I had never encountered a homosexual before.

I decided to nip down to the pub and buy a six-pack, as I knew that he liked his beer. As John began to drink the bottles of beer, he began to relax and he told me his story. He had lived a lonely life as an orphan and sought out other gay men. John had gone to priests of all traditions to hear his confession. With some of them he had had homosexual relations, including several gay Church of Ireland clergy. One of these gay rectors interviewed me for a curacy, but the archbishop would not appoint a single priest under him. The then archbishop is alleged to have kept a black book of the names of wayward clergy.

I told John that the buck stopped here and that he needed to put his life in order. I believe he was bisexual and that he used his homosexuality as a crutch for his loneliness and to attract the attention of lonely gay clergy. I told John that I knew a young woman, Mary, who fancied him. As it happened he was also fond of Mary but he was too shy to ask her out. He eventually plucked up courage and asked her out. I married John and Mary several years afterwards. I visited them in their flat several times, and they were wonderfully happy. They were also blessed with a family. They both died in middle age, but they had enjoyed short years of a happy married life. It may be simplistic but John had come to terms with his human weakness that night in my flat. He was always grateful to me for my ministry, and expressed his thanks whenever I met him.

Another openly gay priest that I knew in the United States was Evans Meek Gregory. He was known as 'the pope Gregory', because he was high church. When I last met him he was chaplain in an Episcopal boys' boarding school in Virginia, USA. I did not think that it was a suitable place for a practising gay priest, for I noticed that the boys were afraid of him. I had visited the school with a clerical friend, Joe Petree, as I had been invited to preach in the school chapel. As Joe and I were travelling together 'the pope' asked us if we wanted to share a bed! Next morning he said that he would marry us if we wished. 'The pope' had performed a number of same sex weddings in Virginia. I was glad to take to the open road, but it was several days before Joe could tell his wife what had happened.

Leeson Park Church in Dublin had been a high profile church with a rector and three curates in the 1920s. It had a reputation for preaching and had produced four bishops that century. Canon Hughes was a most ambitious rector who wanted to be a bishop. When a courier was sent to ask him if he would accept the Bishopric of Kilmore in Co Cavan, Archbishop Gregg of Armagh had a telling comment to make when the courier returned to the Synod Hall and the Episcopal electoral college. 'I'm sure it didn't take him long to make up his mind!' On another occasion Canon Hughes was on his way to a rugby match in Lansdowne Road with his rug under his arm. The sexton had to run after him and tell him that he had a wedding that afternoon.

Victor Dungan, my Rector was a man of great integrity who treated me as a colleague. The glory days of Leeson Park Parish were over, and Victor had a tough task holding a declining parish together. The church is now almost closed as a place of Anglican worship; the big houses had become offices and institutions, and families could no longer afford to live there. The two boarding schools whose pupils attended the church had moved out into the suburbs.

Victor Dungan was a fine organist and musician. An articulate preacher, his presentation was never imaginative. He was fearless at meetings, and never held back expressing the truth. He challenged select vestry members to consider their poor level of giving. He was a man who could have a row one evening, and start the new day afresh. This is a great gift. He was blessed with a hospitable wife, Iris, who never failed to invite me to a lovely lunch most Sundays.

I was now nervous of being single, and did not wish to be approached by any more gays. My life took a new turn when I began to notice an incredibly beautiful young eighteen year old in the church choir. Jean Carlyle was not short on boyfriends, but I began to drop in on Rangers, the senior girl guides where she was a leading member. On another occasion after a social evening, I offered to leave some young people home. I had arranged that I would leave Jean Carlyle home last, and thereby hangs a tale. She invited me to tea one evening but I discovered that she was going to a dress dance with another admirer. She left me with her mother to be entertained! I plucked up courage and invited Jean out to lunch on her nineteenth birthday. We then went on to walk on Killiney beach and I was smitten by this young woman.

My heart fell when Jean chucked her job in insurance and went off to Jersey to work in the Bonne Nuit bay hotel on the north shore of the island. I wrote a few letters and in return she told me that she was having a ball. I did not realise how much I missed her. She arrived home in the Autumn and I brought her to see *Lilac Time* in the Olympia theatre. I then brought her down to Delgany to meet my friend Noel Willoughby who was rector there. The next port of call was my landlady in Belfast. My Mini broke down on the way home and it was pouring rain. I managed to get it to struggle back to Dublin. I proposed to Jean in my landlady's bedroom in Belfast. She accepted.

I realised that I could not bear Jean going out with other men. We met on Christmas Eve and she had a present for me. She did not give it to me, as she did not know how she stood with me. I had the habit of expecting her to be always available when I called and she was fed up with me taking her for granted. I asked her father in an old fashioned way if I could have her hand in marriage. He assented. I had to borrow the money for an engagement ring from my bank manager. Mr Fox, the manager, didn't think it was a good start to married life. Jean was now working in O'Kennedy-Brindley advertising, and did some modelling.

We were married in Christ Church, Leeson Park in September 1962 and honeymooned in Rimini, in Italy. The money for the honeymoon came out of wedding present money. Friend Frank Manning from Malahide sent me a cheque as a wedding present and I wrote that I wouldn't mind receiving presents like his, in duplicate. In London, on the way to Italy I had to go to the bank to get money to pay the hotel bill. The hotelier insisted that we leave our luggage in the hotel until I returned. Italy was a great holiday and we visited Florence and Venice. We ran out of money on our honeymoon.

I was becoming restless in parish life and I wanted to spend more time with young people. I was tired visiting old ladies and drinking afternoon tea. One evening a clergy widow asked me to dinner for 8 pm at the Mespil flats. I gladly accepted, as I was tired of cooking for myself. However I said that I would come at 7 pm as I had a later meeting. I duly arrived at 7 pm and as 8 pm approached there was no sign of food. With that the hostess regretted that I could not stay for dinner and she showed me the door. I was tired of old ladies. Another asked me to collect a bicycle for a jumble sale. When I arrived at her house I found a rusty old bicycle with only one wheel. I was furious as I was being used as a bin collector.

I decided to return to Trinity and study for a higher diploma in education. Shortly afterwards a job became vacant in Saint Andrew's College for an assistant master. I was interviewed by the headmaster, P. J. Southgate, who offered me the post. I was delighted to be appointed. The then Archbishop George Simms, who had sent me a generous cheque on my marriage, wrote me these words when I resigned my curacy: 'Do not forget your ministry.' These were words that I never forgot and which were fulfilled years later. P. J. Southgate wrote a warm letter to me saying that he was delighted that I was exchanging ministry in the parish for ministry in the school. One of my depressing experiences was visiting him near the end of his life. He was in a public ward and had had a leg amputated. It was a traumatic end for this distinguished graduate of Cambridge University.

To a new housemaster, Jim McAleese, Southgate had said that Ruddock played a useful game of ping-pong. It reminded me of the warden of the Divinity Hostel who once told me that at ordination the bishop would hand me a Bible and not a table tennis bat.

I was in charge of cricket at Saint Andrews and we ran a sale at my Blackrock house to fund a cricket coach. One of the items in the sale was a bright check tweed sports coat that Doctor Jackie Wallace of Baggot Street had given me to sell. Jim McAleese bought the jacket and next day as we walked down Baggot Street he suddenly pulled me into Liptons shop. He had seen Jackie Wallace coming towards him and he did not want him to see Jim wearing his old coat. Jim McAleese was a born schoolteacher and a great character. For our cricket sale he arrived in tails and top hat by taxi. In his hands he held a big pot of pancake mix, heavily laced with Guinness! The pancakes were a great success and sold out quickly.

David Evans, the Glamorgan county wicketkeeper, came over from Wales as our cricket coach. As he was about to take a Viscount aircraft at Cardiff he heard of the Aer Lingus Viscount that had gone down in the Irish Sea. His wife pleaded with David not to travel but he came. As well as being a fine coach, David had a wonderful Welsh voice and entertained us at many a party. When his playing days were over he became a county umpire. I last met him after a county game in Sophia Gardens, Cardiff that he was umpiring. David died suddenly and he was a great loss to cricket.

While teaching at Saint Andrews I had to make up my teaching hours at Synge Street Christian Brothers. There I taught French and prepared two classes for Intermediate Certificate. The superior, J. D. Fegan, was a fine educator and he wrote a play on Robert Emmett for the old Abbey at The Queens Theatre in Pearse Street. The Synge Street boys performed the play and it was a great success. I think that it was written for the centenary of the school. I believe that I was the first Higher Diploma student to be paid for teaching. One day the Superior gave me a class list and he asked me to tick off each pupil's homework. There were three or four defaulters. After the Christmas holidays they were gone. I did meet one of them years later when he was a chef in the Shelbourne Hotel, but he bore me no grudge. Synge Street CBS did not accommodate lazy pupils as there was a waiting list. I enjoyed my two years at the school and most of the boys got honours in their exam. They were all so keen to learn. There were one or two sadistic brothers who lived by the strap. They would stand the marked boys at the back of the class. At the end of the class as I looked through the glass partition, I would see the angry brother beating the boys unmercifully with the black strap. I told the boys that I did not approve of the strap or corporal punishment. I never had to send a boy to the superior or put any of them out of class. It was the most satisfying teaching of my career.

It is sad to see the demise of Christian Brothers schools. For years they gave free education to countless generations of boys. There was the custom where each boy brought sixpence each week to school for his education. The brothers were dedicated teachers and gave of their very best. A superior was only elected for five years and this was a good rule, especially if a poor superior was in charge. The brothers have received a bad press but there are always a few bad apples in every barrel.

CHAPTER 12

'God Bless America, land that I love'

While I was teaching I was free to do church locums on Sundays. These visits took me all over the counties Dublin, Kildare, Wicklow and Laois. Sometimes I was invited to lunch and in some parishes I was never asked back to eat. It was while doing duty in Co Kildare that I met a most remarkable Canadian, Garfield Weston. Weston had bought Barrettstown Castle and he had various business interests in Ireland. He had houses around the world. He loved to spend part of the year in Ireland and he was interested in horseracing. He was a devout Christian, attended church when resident and there was an open invitation to lunch each Sunday. He always called me padre, and Mr Weston was shocked to discover that there was no restroom attached to the church. 'What happens if I'm short taken?' Mr Weston asked. I believe that he had a toilet installed in the church. It is incredible that churches restore organs, install new roofs and never think of adding a toilet.

It was at Barretstown Castle that I met Miriam Weston and her husband Charlie Burnett who suffered from Parkinsons disease. They had an only son and they asked me to take him for scripture lessons, which I did. Some years later Miriam invited me out to stay in Florida and to visit Episcopal schools on the east coast. I was put-up in a lovely flat by the seashore in Fort Lauderdale. My travelling expenses were all paid for and when I got off the plane a courier gave me one thousand dollars spending money. It was a huge amount of money and I did not spend it all. I was able to buy a carpet for our living room when I returned home.

In Florida I spent most of my time sunning myself at various pool sides and drinking unending gin and tonics. While husbands were jetting around the world on business, their bored wives spend their time at the pool getting drunk. I met one Irish girl who was a secretary at an Episcopal (Anglican) church. She lived on a diet of Irish whiskey and Irish songs. She was homesick for Ireland and would start crying whenever 'Galway Bay' was sung. When I returned to Ireland she would ring me in a drunken state at any hour of the day or night. She once rang me from Dublin Airport to meet her there, but it was not possible.

Travelling up the east coast I arrived at Richmond, Virginia, near Washington DC. Here I visited Saint Christopher's School where the Weston children had gone to school. Here there was a vacancy for a school chaplain. The headmaster Warren Elmer was open and frank and said that the job was a tough one. On returning to Ireland I was asked to meet the Chairman of the Board who was on holiday in Ireland. I was offered the Chaplain's job and I gave in my notice to Saint Andrew's College. The headmaster Jimmy Duke was kind and offered to give me back my job if America did not work out.

Strike On Here

In 1969 there had been a secondary teachers' strike over poor pay. It was a very bitter strike indeed. I was not a member of the Teachers' Union because clergy were barred from membership. I had a wife and three children to support and it was frustrating to have no say in the strike. Dr Patrick Hillery was Minister of Education and he took a strong line of no surrender. Three teachers on strike went down to Co Wicklow to play golf when a stranger asked them if he could join them. It was only during the round that they discovered that they were playing with their adversary, the Minister of Education. He later became President of Ireland.

I was worried about my income and there was a real fear that teachers would not be paid for the strike period. On a cold winter's night I left the comfort of my home and family for supply teaching in London. I was so lonely leaving my Jean and three daughters. I was so annoyed because I was unemployed due to the decision of others. Next morning I arrived at a freezing Euston Station on a snow covered platform. I headed for my uncle's flat at Camberwell and he offered me a bed while in London. Later that morning I headed for the Eastham Educational Authority in east London to look for supply teaching. I was offered a job at Plaistow Girls School next morning – a tough secondary modern academy.

The teachers there were completely bored with the girls, the school and the drab surroundings. They used to change around the furniture in the staff room each week to relieve the monotony. There was a good deal of racism and one Jewish teacher was called 'Jew Bitch' as she crossed the yard. The girls in the school were from deprived backgrounds and had little or no interest in learning. My job was to stand in for absent teachers. One day I might be teaching English and the next day Domestic Economy. I decided to ask the girls to plan a menu for Claridge's Hotel. Suddenly a girl put up her hand and said that the hotel was not what it was cracked up to be. She had worked in the kitchen there at night. The girls brought no books to school and paper and pencils were given out each morning.

One morning I saw a girl bending down over the desk continually and I went down to investigate. She had pulled her tights down and was repairing them. Some of the girls were half asleep in class and I'm sure that they were 'on the game' at night. One morning the principal asked me to 'patrol' the corridors and I felt like a warder. I was the only teacher who attended the school service in the parish church on Ash Wednesday. The principal was very impressed and offered me a permanent position. The principal had an assistant who was known as MI5 as she was a real spy and reported back everything that went on in the staff room. Each morning for two months I took the tube from Camberwell to Charing Cross and changed for Eastham. Those girls I taught are now middle aged and I often wonder how they fared in life. I will never know.

The teachers' strike dragged on for several months. The teachers at the top of the scale got a big rise while those of us at the bottom of the scale got a few cents a week. The Union Executive was made up of teachers at the top of the scale and their big pay rise offer made them give up the strike. That strike depressed me and I was glad to accept the Chaplain's job in the United States.

A few days before leaving for the United States my youngest daughter caught the measles. She was well enough to travel on New Year's Day 1970. There were many tears at Dublin airport as we set off for London to catch a TWA flight to Dulles Airport outside Washington DC. An Englishman who was teaching at Saint Christopher's School came to collect us in the school station wagon. It was a tiring journey to Richmond, Virginia, but finally we arrived at the house that the school had rented for us. The house was set in a very exclusive neighbourhood with not a black in sight. When our rented house was put on the market a black family stopped out side our drive while I was gardening. They were simply looking for directions. Next door my white racist neighbour was watching intently. I pretended to be showing the black family the house for sale. When the black family had left, my neighbour rushed over to me. I told him that the visitors were interested in buying our house. He nearly had a heart attack. No advertising signs went up when these houses were for sale.

Coming from Ireland I felt an old fashioned conservative. The wealth was alarming, the boys came from affluent homes and many of them had their own cars and chequebooks. Saint Christopher's was a white racist academy. When it was decided to have a token black scholarship, one governor, a surgeon, could not understand how a distinguished school would allow entry 'to the descendant of a black mulatto slave!' When I invited a black priest of a black church to our house for a party, there were embarrassed looks from other white guests. That black priest, Henry Blake, had invited me to preach in his church. When I said how we Irish knew what it was like to be treated as lepers in America, the congregation shouted, 'Amen, brother, alleluia.' When I continued that we Irish built the road and railroads and did the menial work they again shouted 'Amen brother, alleluia.'

I was so innocent that I was not aware that there were drugs on campus. I had a loyal helper in the chapel and I was devastated when it was discovered that he was a drug pusher in the school. He was immediately expelled. There was often tension between myself and the headmaster, Warren Elmer, as he was always sticking his nose in the chapel affairs. He would cancel a chapel service to suit his own programme. When I invited a black panther to speak in chapel I was branded a raving liberal and 'nigger lover'. On another occasion I was almost lynched for inviting a conscientious objector to speak. The most provocative visitor to speak in chapel was the Catholic bishop, who told the boys that they were smug, self-satisfied and lazy looking sods!

Activity period was an exciting event in the school day. It took place once a week after lunch. The whole school assembled to listen to a visiting speaker and then the boys had an opportunity to ask questions. It was a time of violent unrest in America and young men were burning their draft cards. Some of them fled to Canada. The Vietnam War was in full swing and old boys of the school were being killed. The riots in Kent State over the United States entry into Cambodia was a very emotive time. One day as I walked to chapel with a general from the helicopter section of the army he said that he felt a hypocrite speaking to the boys. He believed that Vietnam was a lost cause and that the Vietnamese were not worth fighting for.

I became friendly with one of the teachers, Marc Parrot, and we corresponded for years until his death in Hawaii. Marc was married to Janice, a Chinese lady from Hawaii. He had an unbelievable knowledge of Ireland. One day he asked me why Ben Bulben was called Ben. I told him that I did not know. The flags of all visitor teachers and foreign students hung in the chapel. When I returned to Ireland the Irish flag was taken down. Marc caused a furore and had the flag restored. I often wonder if it still hangs there. Marc was a brilliant English teacher and revered Joyce, Yeats and O'Casey. He became a friend of Saint Patrick's and he treasured a letter from the Dean of Saint Patrick's Cathedral, Dublin. He and Janice came to Ireland and I was delighted to be able to show them Wexford.

A Good Man

The co-adjutor Bishop of Virginia was Bob Hall. A co-adjutor bishop has the right to succeed the diocesan bishop. It was always a mystery to me how a liberal from a church in Chicago was appointed to conservative Virginia. One of his sons had a problem with drugs. Bishop Bob had a problem with alcohol and one day at a clergy gathering he said: 'Gentlemen I am an alcoholic.' His honesty was uplifting and he had all our love, sympathy and support. He was such a contrast to the stuffiness of Virginians.

'My son, my son'

Our social life in Richmond, Virginia, centred around the swimming pool at the diocesan retreat centre. I got cheap membership of the squash racket club, where I played a lot of competitive squash. I also played squash around the state and in the state championships. We were invited to cocktail parties which were formal affairs.

My wife Jean was bored as the three girls were at school and play school. The solution to that problem was the birth of our son Norman Carlyle in December 1970. By then we decided that we were homesick for Ireland and in early 1971 we booked our passage home for the summer on board the QE 2. I had always wanted to travel on this liner and now my dream was being fulfilled.

Our five days on the QE 2 were heaven, but losing an hour each day it was hard to wake up in the mornings. It was difficult to eat all the food. We were not used to seven course breakfasts. Strangely enough the only church on the ship was a Jewish synagogue. It was no more expensive to travel by ship than air. There were then 2.40 dollars to the pound and our trip for two adults and four children was five hundred pounds.

In the early days of the century the British fleet anchored in Cobh harbour. It was the port for many transatlantic liners and many countries had consulates there. It is also the resting place of many of the *Lusitania* dead. On a summer's morning in 1971 we disembarked from the QE 2 and took the tender to Cobh harbour. There on the platform were Jean's parents, who had never seen their first grandson, and my sisters Daphne and Gladys. It was good to be home.

I had arrived back in Ireland with no money in the bank. All my savings had been spent on travelling home on the QE 2. I had accepted a teaching job in Gonzaga College, a Jesuit school in Ranelagh in Dublin. A friend of my sister's had put in a good word for me with the principal and I was offered a post teaching French. It was tough work as my French was rusty. I was also appointed games master. This was a difficult assignment as none of other teachers helped with games. I had to take rugby, but hockey was my first love. It was almost impossible to get the Jesuit priests to bring teams away to other schools, especially on Saturdays.

Gonzaga was an exclusive school for the well off Catholics and Dublin 4 Fine Gaelers. The names Fitzgerald and Costello figured prominently. The morning after Bloody Sunday I was given the cold shoulder and for some reason I was identified with the aggressor. The boys seemed to side with the Catholic rebels whose aim was to usurp the institutions of the state. I was hurt by the polarisation of the boys. Somehow they seemed to see me on the same side as the British paratroops. One boy said, 'You're not Irish, you're British.' I wondered if Tommy Toyota born of Japanese parents in Belfast was any less an Irishman than Paddy O'Reilly from Kerry who worked on London building sites? I felt in Gonzaga that I was a stranger in a different cultural environment. The school was not unlike the American school where I taught with the same levels of affluence. There were some fine teaching colleagues there, among them Ray Kearns and John Wilson. Ray, a distinguished Maths teacher founded the successful Institute of Education in Leeson Street and was very generous when one of my daughters attended courses there. John Wilson, a classical scholar became a TD, and Minister of Education. He was a warm friendly and encouraging man. He was also a very approachable government minister.

CHAPTER 13

'Do Not Forget Your Ministry'

I began to feel a real desire to be back in fulltime ministry. I remembered the words written by Archbishop Simms when I took up teaching. They were prophetic words: 'Do not forget your ministry.' When I was teaching at Saint Andrew's College I helped Canon Ernest Bateman, who was a superb preacher, in his church at Booterstown. He was a man of great courage who took on the primary teachers' union when he appointed a woman principal, Kathleen Blake. He also had to deal with aggressive parishioners when his daughter church, Carysfort was closed. When the canon retired he asked an old lady in the street how the new man was getting on. 'Oh Canon, he doesn't hold me the way you used to!' Canon Bateman was a fund of fun. In the vestry one morning before service he asked the organist why Ruddock wore blue braces. 'To hold his trousers up, woman!' The canon and I had a great relationship, and when he was retiring he told me to select any books I wanted out of his library. Canon Bateman loved the ministry, and his influence made me consider the parochial ministry again.

I decided to retire from fulltime teaching and wait for a suitable clerical appointment. During those months I painted houses, sold fruit from the market and went around door-to-door selling carpet shampoo. It was called Swipe. I did very well selling the carpet shampoo.

In January 1973 I was appointed rector of Killane and Killegney, near Enniscorthy in Co Wexford. Here our four children had a wonderful childhood in a modern rectory looking out on the Blackstairs Mountains. There were plenty of children of the same age there. As the next generation abandoned farming there are now fewer children.

When I went for interview with Bishop McAdoo at the Palace, Kilkenny, he berated me for being five minutes late for lunch. I had driven from Dublin through heavy morning traffic, and felt like giving him a kick in the you know where. McAdoo could be so pompous. One of the most comical moments with McAdoo was at a clergy lunch hosted by himself. I told him that the stew was good. 'Norrie (my pet name) it's not stew, it's goulash,' he retorted. Growing up I was called Norrie. I didn't like the name much as a girl in the parish was called Norrie. I told the stew story to Archbishop Bill Burnett of Capetown. He was invited to McAdoo's for lunch. Stew was on the menu, but McAdoo was in bed with a cold. Burnett complimented Mrs McAdoo on the goulash. She said, 'Oh it's not goulash, it's just stew!'

After my interview in Kilkenny I drove over the Blackstairs Mountains to meet the parish nominators and then on to meet the diocesan nominators. The nominators appoint rectors to parishes, unlike the Roman Catholic system where the bishop makes the appointments. The local nominators depressed me, as they had no vision for the parish. They simply wanted me to take Sunday services and visit the sick. They told me that the parish was 'very snug' financially. Over the next eight years they were to discover that ministry was more than the minimum.

The next stop on the interview trail was to visit the Dean of Ferns, Tom McFall. Tom was a distinguished country gentleman who was not dependent on a clergy salary. As the deanery was an enormous mansion a dean had to be found with private means. He married a lady 'with old money', and he fitted the bill. When Dean McFall arrived in St Stephen's Green outside his club and emerged from his expensive car in gaiters and frock coat, the car park attendant addressed him as 'My Lord!' The car park attendant was well rewarded for his courtesy. Now the attendants are no more. McFall told me that I was mad to be giving up teaching to become a rector. This was not encouraging.

The last stop on my whistle stop tour was a visit to the archdeacon in Gorey. I asked Parker if I would have enough work to do in the vacant parish. 'You won't be in top gear, but occasionally you'll be in third,' he said. Some years later when I was dealing with difficult parishioners, he told me the story of the fish exporter who was exporting fresh salmon to Fishguard. When the fish reached Fishguard they were all dead. For the next journey he put a pike in the tank and the fish all arrived live. 'The pike keeps you on your toes, Norman!' Parker replied.

The Blackstairs valley from Bunclody in North Wexford to Clonroche in the southeast is an enclave of traditional Church of Ireland farmers. Clonroche has the richest soil in Ireland, if not in Europe. Those in the lowlands had big farms, while those nearer the Blackstairs Mountains had much smaller farms which were not very fertile.

One generous farmer kept us supplied with central heating oil. One day the AIB bank manager asked me to call. He informed me that a number of my parishioners had lodged money in the bank toward our children's boarding fees. This generosity was humbling as they too were paying substantial fees for their own children. This generosity was repeated for a number of years, which greatly eased our financial worries. Education is one of the problems of living in the country. We were kept well supplied with vegetables and fruit and at Christmas we received a big expensive hamper from the parish. I sowed strawberries in my small plot and the children helped to pick them in the summer. They all worked throughout the summers picking fruit and supervising at the fruit processors nearby. It taught them the value of money. When the fruit season ended, we headed off to Kerry most years for the month of August. These were wonderful holidays. Sometimes I did locums when accommodation was supplied and other years we camped.

While we were living in Co Wexford our daughter Karen won the Young Scientists Exhibition at the Royal Dublin Society in Dublin. She had previously won several category prizes and now she had taken the top prize. Her project was a very comprehensive study of lichens. One of the judges rang us in Clonroche to tell us that Karen was the Young Scientist of 1980 and that the award would be made that evening. We all jumped into the car and headed for Dublin filled with excitement. The Minister of Education, John Wilson, presented Karen with her trophy. During the exhibition Charlie Haughey, the Taoiseach, visited the stands with Frank Dunlop, his spin-doctor, in attendance. When I was introduced to Haughey he said that Karen must have had a good-looking mother. Karen went on to win the European Young Scientists competition in Amsterdam. Aer

Lingus, the then sponsors, gave us free tickets to Amsterdam. Doctor Carmel Sharkey, Karen's science teacher travelled with us. Carmel taught at Alexandra College and took a personal interest in Karen's project. I am sure that Carmel contributed to Karen's success.

Karen received a trophy from a local Co Wexford Catholic School. A school Principal of a Catholic Secondary School in Co Laois sent Karen a warm letter of congratulations and a generous cheque. Enniscorthy Urban Council gave her a civic reception. My father, who spent his working life in the town, would have been delighted. Karen went on to study Applied Linguistics and spent years teaching in Japan. She returned to lecture in Japanese at Trinity College and is presently completing a doctorate.

In the parish there was an annual collection for church funds and peoples' arms were twisted to give. Others were made to feel guilty for not giving. I could not go along with this begging because I believe that the Lord supplies. When the issue was raised at a vestry meeting (parish council), the treasurer spitting fire shouted that it was mad to think that the Lord would provide. He walked out of the meeting and a strange peace descended on the room. A miracle happened, because the floodgates opened and the money poured in. If you see a mean parish you will find a mean treasurer. The parish began to give away large sums to charities each year and was never in need. There is a sign over a school in Virginia, USA which says, 'Help us to remember that what we keep we lose, and only what we give remains our own.' That treasurer who walked out of the meeting resigned and he only spoke to me once again in this life. It was Easter Day and as I put my hand out to wish him a Happy Easter he said, 'Get away from me, get away from me, don't touch me.' You can't win them all.

There was little social intercourse between Roman Catholics and members of the Church of Ireland. When my wife Jean decided to start a Brownie pack for girls, open to all faiths and none, there was certain opposition. She rode the storm and it provided an open forum for all the young girls in the community to meet, play and pray together.

One of the most amusing incidents took place at a Girl Guide

camp near Clonroche, Co Wexford. It was decided to have an ecumenical communion service with the Reverend Aidan Jones
and myself participating. Aidan was then the youth officer for
the Diocese of Ferns and a committed ecumenist. We decided
that we would ask the Roman Catholic guides to form a line for
their sacrament and the Church of Ireland guides a second line.
After the service Aidan and myself noticed one of the young
guides crying. 'I've swallowed Protestant bread,' she cried. She
had joined the wrong queue! Aidan immediately consoled her
and gave her absolution. It brought home to us the tragedy of
our divisions.

Before a harvest festival an ignorant farmer warned me to beware of what I said at the service, because 'there were some of
them here tonight!' At a healing service in the same church some
years later a Roman Catholic nun in her eighties wept. She had
never been in a Church Of Ireland church before and all her life
she had felt bitter because of the plantations. Her family had
been evicted from their land. The nun had a great healing that
day and her resentment had been washed away.

A wise old farmer, Willie Tector of Clonroche, pulled me
aside one day and gave me sound advice: 'Don't let anyone pull
you out of the saddle.' I had an amusing incident with Willie
Tector one day when I met him in Molloy Murphy's pub. I had
gone in to buy stamps when the post office was closed for the
half day. There I saw Willie sitting at the bar. He was embarrassed. What should I do? If I walked out he would think that I
was judging him. I decided to buy him a drink. 'What will you
have Willie?' 'A double brandy, your reverence!' I was broke for
a week afterwards.

Years later I met the parish secretary who had since moved
away. He is a lovely person, but he still remembers the acrimo-
nious vestry meetings, dominated by a few bullyboy farmers.
One gentle farmer refused to serve on vestries because of the
rows. What a commentary on church life. An Anglo Irish lady in
the midlands loved rows at vestry meetings because it made
them more exciting! I was a liberal in the midst of conservative
Fine Gaelers.

One of the great characters in Clonroche was John Jude
Doyle of the Cloughban Inn. He was the only capitalist labour

member in the community. One night John Jude and myself set out to tour the pubs and houses, as we were collecting funds to build a new Community Workshop in New Ross. Our first port of call was Molly Murphy's pub. John Jude like a good publican stood a round to all who were there. Molly gave us a half a crown (about 15 cents). 'Nor, if this carries on we're going to lose money,' John said. There was a great response by the farming community to the Community Workshops, which were built and continue to flourish.

John Jude invited me to the labour party dinner in Wexford and the guest speaker was Brendan Corish TD, then Minister of Health. The booze flowed and on the following week my picture was on the front page of *The Echo* with Corish and the labour party stalwarts. The parishioners were not amused. I was politically innocent. When Erskine Childers was running for President I felt that it would be a tragedy if such an outstanding politician was not elected. I proceeded to stick up Fianna Fáil posters on the windows of my car in support of Childers. Some days later I received anonymous phone calls. My car would be burnt if I did not remove the posters. I took them down and I was delighted when Erskine Childers was elected President of Ireland. I met Erskine in Castlegregory when I was taking services in Co Kerry. He came to church and sat in the back seat. I took the service because the local rector was too nervous to preach in the presence of the President. President Childers was a most gracious man and I have warm memories of him in Co Kerry. Tragically he died too early in office.

There was little or no mixing between the Roman Catholic and Church of Ireland school children in Clonroche. The two schools had no contact whatsoever. Courtnacuddy School did make contact with Killegney Church of Ireland School and I remember a joint sports day. Clonroche School had to close because there was a serious outbreak of measles. Not one child in the Church of Ireland School contracted measles. This was sure proof of the social apartheid between the two schools and communities. Another telling incidence of tribalism was when I brought the body of a Scottish solicitor to church on a Saturday evening. Next morning when parishioners came to church they were fearful when they entered the church. Who was dead?

There was relief when it was discovered that the dead man was 'only a blow in'. Another time there was serious violence in a home. It was so serious that we took mother and children in to our home. A local parishioner told me not to worry about these people as they were only 'blow ins' from England and not one of us.

Before I came to live in Clonroche I was told that this was the murder village in Co Wexford. The tragedy concerned the murder of a local school teacher's daughter and the murder enquiry went on for a long time. Finally the case broke wide open, a local man in the village confessed to the murder and he was sent to Mountjoy jail. The murderer died in prison and I happened to be out in the garden when his remains were being brought to the chapel. Nobody followed the hearse. In death the murderer was totally rejected as he had brought shame on the village. His widow had changed her name to Mrs Maddox – her maiden name. She often babysat for us. The trauma of the murder lived with her for the remainder of her life. We were very upset when she was committed to the local mental hospital. When we went to visit her she cried bitterly. As the door locked behind her she continued to cry bitterly. We wanted to take her home with us. Mrs Maddox died shortly afterwards, and I believe she died of a broken heart.

Dick Binions, a farmer treasurer who had little formal education, kept financial books accurate to the last cent. Before I came to the parish he told me that it was 'very snug financially'. One day I met him in the bank and as he was doing business I whispered to him jokingly, 'lay not up for yourselves treasures on earth'. Years later he knocked on the vestry door as I was preparing to conduct a service. He handed me a very generous personal cheque for my use. Dick said that he had never forgotten my words in the bank that day. It's amazing how innocent words can bear fruit.

A brother of Dick was married to the local schoolteacher. The brother told me that a man had no problems 'when he was lying with his back to the government at night'. It is strange how many poor or broken down farmers married national school teachers. Now that rural schools have closed that lucrative supply of wives had dried up.

CHAPTER 14

The Fire Fell

It was at the end of the seventies that I came in contact with the charismatic movement. I had become stale in my ministry and needed fresh outlook. The charismatic movement was a movement of the Holy Spirit which longed to see new life in all the churches. It also sought to revive in the church the gifts and fruits of the Spirit. The movement had spread rapidly across all the churches in the United States. A book written by an Anglican priest, Dennis Bennett, *Nine O'clock in the Morning*, tells the story of how Bennett was filled with the Spirit and new life. Father Francis McNutt, a Roman Catholic priest in the US developed a huge healing ministry. He spoke at an international charismatic conference in the RDS in Dublin in front of a number of cardinals headed by Cardinal Suenens of Belgium. Cardinal Suenens had pioneered the charismatic movement in the Roman Catholic Church and written books on the subject. A conservative Catholic, seeing the happy crowds streaming out of the RDS charismatic conference, shouted 'citadel of Satan'.

Prayer groups began to spring up all over Ireland, many ecumenical in character. The Roman Catholic Church felt that the charismatic movement was becoming too ecumenical, and strong pressure was exerted to keep it Roman Catholic. Inter communion became another divisive issue.

Whenever there is new life in the church, evil is near at hand.

Evil was brought home to me when a young teenage girl started coming to a parish prayer meeting. When the Bishop of Singapore spoke in her school she became a different person, shouting and screaming. The bishop ministered to her. When she came to the next meeting at the rectory her whole personality changed and she had the strength of a grown man. I ministered to her, pointing a crucifix at her. She then moved into a corner of the room and her face was the face of evil. This was a case for a deliverance ministry. The girl was strangely possessed. Some nights later Father Bob Staples, a Roman Catholic priest, and myself visited the girl's home to minister to her. She exhibited the same behaviour again, and again the crucifix subdued her. She seemed to recover from this entire trauma, but I firmly believe that she met evil somewhere, or in another person.

One of my classmates in the Divinity School, the Reverend Cecil Kerr, had given up the chaplaincy at Queen's University to live on faith in a house of prayer in Rostrevor. This move greatly inspired me as a colleague launched out into the deep. Cecil funnelled many overseas visitors down to our Wexford parish where a group of parishioners longed to take their Christianity more seriously and where worship was coming alive. I arranged a charismatic conference in White's Hotel and Cecil Kerr came to speak. He spoke of the valley of dry bones in the book of Ezekiel. 'Can these bones live?' was the question that we examined that day. I had booked the hotel not knowing who would pay for it. A retiring collection paid the bill many times over. I arranged a conference for Church of Ireland clergy at Horetown House to look at renewal in the church and the restoration of the gifts of the Spirit – wisdom, knowledge, healing, miracles, speaking in tongues. Clergy with real needs came from all over Ireland. Bishop John Armstrong who identified strongly with the charismatic movement came, as did Walton Empey and his wife. Walton was then Dean of Limerick and had been moved by The Fisherfolk, a music group who lived in community in England. Shortly afterwards many of us there that weekend attended an international leaders' conference in Canterbury. Over thirty Anglican bishops attended and our final act of worship in Canterbury Cathedral was a wonderful act of joy to be in the presence of the Lord. The bishops at the end of the service danced before the altar. The news spread worldwide.

Charismatic speakers found their way to our door in Clonroche – nuns from Tanzania, Jesuits from South Africa, Methodists from the US and many more. Joe Petree from North Carolina was a real prophet. He had been a pastor in the mountains of North Carolina and had invited a black speaker to his church. When he arrived with his speaker at the church on Sunday morning a mob of parishioners had already arrived with guns and ropes. A lynching was on the cards. The local sheriff put Joe and his black visitor in the squad car, picked up Joe's wife and three daughters at the rectory, and left town. It has been too painful an experience for Joe ever to return to that community.

On a 'visit' to our home Joe noticed that I was burnt out. He said very prophetic words: 'You can't change the direction of a mule that is lying down.' Those words encouraged me to plan for my future life. At that time we were experiencing the highs of religious experience. However, the charismatic movement had many weaknesses. It seemed to have little apostolate to the world and to the social needs of society. It may well have been a holy huddle of the like minded.

One of the most amazing visitors was Big Jim White who spent his life as a Pentecostal, ministering in the Yukon of Canada to miners. He told us the fascinating story of sitting in an oncologist's waiting room with other cancer patients. Sitting beside him was a black lady. Turning to her he said, 'If we're to survive, sister, we had better lay hands on one another.' He later did research and they were the only two patients to survive. Before Big Jim left he made me promise that I would always lay hands on the sick. I have tried to carry out that promise.

It was at this stage in the late seventies that my daughters came in contact with a dynamic young people's church group, called Shalom. They met in an old castle in Templeogue near Dublin. The group were led by a unique couple, Chris and Lillian Rowe, who lived totally on faith. They had no interest in material things and Chris drove a battered old car. Lillian's parents had been missionaries in China. Bono of U2 was a member of the group and spoke at a memorial service for Lillian. Many of these young people are now missionaries in different parts.

I am writing these words next door to the Loreto College where Shalom conducted a lively and inspirational day of worship one Sunday. The Loreto School hall was packed out. On another occasion Shalom brought the Christian rock band, Living Sound, to the Castle Ballroom in Enniscorthy. Again the concert was booked out.

Shalom is now no more and all those young people are now middle aged. It had a profound influence on one generation of

youth, and I shall never forget its vitality. The charismatic movement has also lost its vitality and very little remains of its life. In
the course of the church's history there come times of great revival and evangelism. Then these times die away to revive again
years later. In the early church the early Christians were accused
of being drunk when the Holy Spirit fell on them. 'How can they
be drunk, it is only nine o'clock in the morning?' 'The fire fell.'
Those words are written over a church in the North of England
where a rector, the Reverend Alexander Boddy, was filled with
the Spirit and where his congregation was renewed. The south
of Wales is filled with numerous chapels, now closed. These
grew up through the great religious revival in Wales in 1903, but
the revival has long since past.

What of the churches today? They spend their time dealing
with sex abuse and scraping the diocesan barrels to pay com-
pensation to the victims of abuse. The churches have lost their
way, lost the confidence and respect of the people they are here
to serve. Their energies are spent preaching the gospel of predictability and seem to have forgotten about evangelism. Will
we see a renewal of church life and witness in our lifetime? I
pray that we will. Otherwise more and more churches and
chapels will be padlocked forever. The fire needs to fall again to
burn up the intrigue, the cover-ups, the abuse of power in
ecclesiastical institutions. We may live to see that day.

CHAPTER 15

O Bishop Divine

During the seventies I served under three bishops in the diocese of Ferns – McAdoo, Armstrong and Willoughby. A previous bishop, John Percy Phair whom I had known since childhood, ordained me a priest in Saint Canice's Cathedral, Kilkenny in 1959. I spent the pre-ordination retreat with the bishop at the Palace in Kilkenny and he was a gracious host. I was in a bedroom on the top floor of the Palace and the uniformed maid brought me up an enamel jug of hot water in the morning to wash and shave. The bishop delivered a number of talks in the chapel and I still remember his talks. He focused on the Greek word *doulos*, a slave. The slave shackled in the depths of the galley ship rowed in the intense heat. It was the most menial task of all. The priest, the bishop said, is called to the most menial service, and needs to forget about pride and status.

His successor Bishop McAdoo came from Cork where he had been Dean of Saint Fin Barre's Cathedral. When he was appointed dean he met a school friend in Patrick's Street, Cork who addressed him as Harry. 'Mr Dean, please,' he replied. McAdoo could be very aloof. When I rang him to ask if I could bring some schoolchildren to see the Palace he said it was a ridiculous suggestion. Shortly afterwards he rang to say that his wife had scolded him and of course we could come. He had a very good way with children and made them very welcome that day.

Another day he would not stop to discuss the problems of a poor widow after a meeting. He said that I seemed to have a lot of problem parishioners and he was tired. He wanted to get back to Kilkenny for his dinner. If the bishop was not concerned about my problems why should I worry. That widow's husband had stuck his head in a gas oven. Next morning at 9.00 am he rang to apologise and listened to the full story. He gave the case every support. His apology said much about the man.

One organist, Mabel, was a very evangelical Christian and she had little time for bishops in fine robes. If there had been a Baptist church nearby I believe she would have gone there. Mabel got word that the bishop was coming, and told me that she would not play the organ that Sunday. Eventually I explained to her that that the bishop was not so bad and she agreed to play. Bishop McAdoo arrived early that Sunday morning and greeted the organist warmly. She brushed by him without saying a word. 'Your organist is not very friendly,' the bishop said. 'Well, bishop, she does not approve of bishops,' I replied. He was taken aback.

McAdoo was a man with great *authoritas*, who was every inch a prelate. A visitor arrived at his door one day and told the bishop that he had read all his books. The visitor said he was a priest and McAdoo invited him for dinner. The visitor asked if he could celebrate Holy Communion in the nearby cathedral next morning. The bishop rang the dean who readily agreed. Weeks later the bogus priest appeared in court in Dublin for bouncing cheques. The judge asked him if anyone could speak on his behalf and he said Bishop McAdoo in Kilkenny. The bogus priest had been in prison where he read McAdoo's books.

McAdoo was my bishop for four short years and was appointed Archbishop of Dublin. At his last service in Saint Canice's Cathedral he confirmed my eldest daughter Karen.

John'll Fix It

McAdoo's successor in Kilkenny was John Armstrong. He was Bishop of Cashel, Waterford and Lismore and with McAdoo's departure his diocese was joined to Ossory, Ferns and Leighlin. Armstrong did not want to move into the Palace and delayed moving house. McAdoo said that Armstrong had 'a villa mentality'! Armstrong did not enjoy good health. He had diabetes and poor circulation. He also had the unfortunate habit of falling asleep at meetings and waking up when they were nearly over.

Bishop John was present at our rectory at a meeting the day before the election of a new archbishop of Armagh. We laid hands on him. Next day he was elected to Armagh, much to his surprise. His one great gift was availability and he was always there to meet people. He was known as 'John'll fix it'. He once promised to fix the appointment of a deanery for one of his clergy but he had already promised it to two others. Armstrong didn't always fix it, and he could not be trusted about appointments. Years before, he offered me a post in Saint Patrick's Cathedral, but I never heard anymore from him. Years later at a retreat in Co Wexford I collared him after lunch as I felt resentful towards him. He told me that he had been forced to give my job to a redundant headmaster by a persuasive bishop.

John Armstrong was a lonely man and always in need of affirmation. He was most annoyed when I resigned from his monthly think tank, as I could not go along with the co-ordinator. Shortly afterwards he visited the parish and asked me after the service if he had done okay. I said 'yes'. 'Then you haven't totally rejected me,' he replied. I cried at his formal funeral. He would have loved something more intimate and personal.

Noel Willoughby, Archdeacon of Dublin, came to Ferns as our bishop in 1980. He was a unanimous choice and a native of Kilpipe in Co Wicklow, one of our own. He had few equals as a pastoral bishop and this added to a fine brain and buckets of earthy wisdom paved the way for an effective ministry among us. He loved the Palace, and there was strong pressure from the Representative Church Body to dispose of the house. He demanded the keys of the Palace and informed the chief officer of the Church Body that if he did not have a positive response by 4 pm next day that he would not accept the bishopric. The Church Body backed down and Bishop Noel made the house a very welcoming open door. Noel was aware of the pressure to dispose of the house and not long before he retired he called a meeting of both diocesan councils. It was unanimously agreed, I believe, to retain the Palace as the bishop's residence.

Bishop Noel had a great rapport with the whole community. I canvassed strongly to have Noel elected as a Freeman of Wexford and I was delighted when he was elected. He also conducted the last retreat at Saint Kieran's seminary, Kilkenny before it closed down. Noel had a great gift of putting pen to paper to remember special events in his clergy's lives. I treasure the letter and cheque that he sent me when I resigned my parish. My Archdeacon, William Parker, told me that the bishop cried when I left.

CHAPTER 16

The Open Road

After eight years in rural Wexford I had itchy feet to move on. I felt that I had stayed too long but I did not receive any invitations to move elsewhere. I decided to fast for the forty days of Lent in 1981. In the Bible when people fasted there were startling results. I lived on a diet of soup, coffee and a marvellous multi vitamin pill called Vivioptal. During the forty days fast my doctor, Barry O'Meara, examined me several times to check that my health was okay. Many people felt that I was mad to fast, but I felt I had to do it. I kept a private diary of each day of the fast. On April 1st – the twenty ninth day of the fast I wrote in my diary: 'April Fool's Day – a fool for Christ's sake. Some power outside myself tried to make me give up my prayer and fasting. I felt nauseous in a way that I had never felt before – a kind of sickly death. I felt all my strength draining from me. We read that the evil one left Jesus. He could not conquer him. I have now lost some weight and I now weigh eleven stone five pounds. Richard Foster in his book, *Celebration of Discipline*, wrote that the stomach is an indulgent spoiled child.'

One of my old teaching colleagues in Richmond Virginia, Marc Parrott, wrote to me from his retirement home in Hawaii, and enclosed a cheque for the Bobby Sands fund. Sands was one of the republican prisoners in Long Kesh prison who died after a long fast. I decided not to send the money to the Sands fund and instead I bought a pair of walking boots. In the middle of the Sands fast I did a trial walk to New Ross, some fifteen miles away. I got severe blisters. This was practice for a long walk on the open road, for I had decided to walk to Northern Ireland as a pilgrimage for peace.

I had been offered a castle in Co Meath as a retreat centre. Without any consultation with my wife and children, I resigned my parish. I know that my bishop, Noel Willoughby, was very disappointed at this news.

I decided to walk as far as Downpatrick where I had been invited to preach in the cathedral. There was also a gathering there that Pentecost Sunday of Christians from all over Ireland.

I was exhausted after walking twenty to thirty miles a day but I felt a great sense of freedom out on the open road. Bishop Walton Empey, who had walked from Limerick to Dublin, advised me to carry a stick to ward off dogs. This was good advice. One of the most unpleasant features was the whiplash from lorries when they passed. I stayed with friends each night and only had to use a hotel on one night in Drogheda. I generally walked along the back roads though I walked on the main road from Drogheda to the border.

I decided to walk the coast road from Newry to Rostrevor where my college friend Cecil Kerr gave me a bed. Next morning I set off from Rostrevor with ex-priest Eugene Boyle to walk to Downpatrick. Near Newcastle in Co Down I passed a group of fundamentalist Christians, clad in dark clothes. They asked me if I was saved. I laughed. Eugene was walking behind me and heard their question. He said to the group: 'You asked my friend if he was saved. He has walked one hundred and eighty miles, but you didn't ask him if he was hungry or thirsty?'

The castle retreat centre project did not materialise. The owner had his own ideas for its future use and I did not think I would have a free reign. When other Christians were offered the castle it did not work out either. I was well out of it.

Here I was with no income and a family of six to support. I worked part time in a Dublin parish but I found it all too sedate and predictable. It was then that I met Neal Carlin, a priest who had been trained in St Peter's seminary, Wexford. We first met at a conference in Rostrevor, Co Down.

Neal and I, under the auspices of Prison Fellowship, used to visit Magilligan prison. There we ministered to a group of prisoners of all traditions. It took great courage for the inmates to step outside the tribe. One prisoner had had a jam jar smashed into his face for attending the prayer meeting. Several others had been beaten. I knew the governor of the prison, Bob Gibson, who had attended Trinity College, trained for the Presbyterian ministry, but later entered the prison service. It was a politically sensitive post.

In 1982 I took the bus regularly to Derry to go into Magilligan prison under the auspices of Prison Fellowship. The fellowship had been founded by Chuck Colson of Watergate notoriety in the Richard Nixon government. Colson had served a prison sentence and when he was released he decided to start a ministry to prisoners around the world. He came to speak in Ireland and he spoke with great feeling and commitment.

Magilligan prison stands close to the seashore, near Ballykelly, the scene of a horrific bombing. It's a strange place with no grass, no trees and no bird song. It had a Mars like appearance. The number of gates you pass through to reach the H Blocks leave you totally disorientated. Inside each H Block there is a board with prisoners' names, date of entry and date of release. No board was more depressing – John Doe, entry 1980, dates of release 2010. These men had committed a kind of political adultery – love of country had replaced love of wife and family. Incarceration led to the breakdown of marriage and many wives had moved in with friends of their imprisoned husbands. These husbands, in theory, might be in prison for the next thirty years. The prison officers did not take kindly to a Catholic priest and a Church of Ireland clergyman ministering together. One evening as we passed by a group of warders one whispered behind the priest 'Catholic bastard'! Another evening in the canteen the food was almost thrown at us.

It was while moving around Northern Ireland with my Catholic priest friend, Neal Carlin that I saw the subtlety of bigotry. Neal and I were driving back to Derry one evening from Magilligan prison when we were stopped at a roadblock. 'Where are you going?' the policeman with rifle asked aggressively. 'To Derry', said Neal. The policeman shouted to his mate in the ditch, 'Ever heard of fucking Derry Jack'? 'Never,' Jack replied. In exasperation, Fr Neal replied, 'We're going to the city.' Grudgingly we were allowed to continue our journey. I had experienced naked sectarianism. When I offered a family member, born in the South of Ireland, Neal's book to read, *Freedom to the Captives,* he refused when he saw 'Derry' on the cover, rather than Londonderry. Londonderry speaks of the unionist description of the city; Derry speaks of the nationalist side. Using the name of the city puts people into one of two camps. However, for centuries the diocese was known as the diocese of Derry and the bishop, the bishop of Derry.

On my visits to Magilligan prison I came to know some of the prisoners who met for our ecumenical prayer meeting. I treasure a letter from Pat McCann of 'C Wing, H Block 3'. He wrote to me, 'Remember I was telling you of the wife and child and us not seeing each other for over a year? Well out of the blue she has asked for a visit. There's a Class A pass for her in a fortnight's time. I think the Spirit is pointing out that I'm as much to blame as she is.' Of his imprisonment Pat wrote, 'I'm here, maybe God has a reason for me being here as no way could I have found him outside, so it's not a bad thing this has happened. There's a far wiser man going to walk out than came in. So maybe I've found something that money could never buy. Right here in this prison faith and love, two things I'd never any time for, Norman. So thanks, Jesus, for giving us such dear precious brothers like Norman. We are all the same body.'

Pat McCann was one who found faith in Magilligan Prison and a reason for living. As I told some of the dubious prisoners – you can hate everything I stand for, but you can't stop me loving you. Twenty-five years on, I wonder where he is now, and what he is doing. It took great courage for the prisoners to leave their own tribal H Block, and come to our prayer meetings.

The Trip of Tensions

In 1982 four of us clergy decided to take a trip around Ireland speaking on reconciliation. There were two Roman Catholic priests, Neal Carlin from Derry and Frank McCloskey from Albany, New York. The other was a Methodist, Joe Petree from North Carolina, and myself.

Frank McCloskey, the American priest, was a very loud, egocentric. He arrived for the trip in American fashion with bumper stickers to sell. We refused to let him hawk these stickers around Ireland. Frank had one great introductory story to his talks. Thousands of ants were under a golf ball. As the golfer swung the club he missed the ball and killed a couple of thousand ants. Eventually, after many misses only two ants remained under the ball. One said to the other, 'If we're to survive we had better get on the ball.'

There were great tensions as we four 'kings' travelled from town to town. When we spoke we had a method of telling the speaker when he was going on too long. We would start putting our foot on the brakes like the brake of a train engine, moving our feet forwards and backwards. It worked. At times we had to make a great effort to keep travelling together. Neal was a wild driver and nearly crashed the car. There was at times great tension and anger among us and we realised that the tensions and divisions of Ireland were within ourselves.

'Drogheda Remembered'
It was then that I received an invitation from the Peace and Justice Commission of the Roman Catholic diocese of Albany, New York to preach at a Mass of Reconciliation on the 3rd anniversary of Pope John Paul's visit to Drogheda in Ireland. This service took place in the Cathedral in Albany, the state capital, and it was a great occasion. Both Catholic and Episcopalian (Anglican) bishops were present and it was a joy to see the Catholic bishop give his Episcopalian colleague the wafer at communion.

From Albany, New York, I travelled down by Amtrak to Greensboro, North Carolina. There we stayed with the Reverend Joe Petree. Joe had a great love for Ireland, had visited it many times and had travelled around the world taking missions with Fr Francis McNutt, the healing priest, Fr Jim Burke a Dominican priest and Faith Smith, a woman with a very prophetic ministry. Joe is a very prophetic person who found it difficult to conform to his Methodist bishop or superintendent. One occasion Joe met the local alcoholic who was rejected in the community – he bought him a drink. Years later he met the alcoholic again and he was 'dry'. He told Joe that he stopped drinking because Joe had accepted him as he was so many years ago. Look what would happen if we exercised acceptance.

It was during these three years on the open road that I spent two summers in Killarney, helping a friend run a bookshop and newsagent's. Mike had worked in South America with the Holy Ghost fathers, but had never been ordained. He had the wisdom to marry a wonderful psychotherapist from Cork, Angela McAdoo. Angela's father was a first cousin of Bishop McAdoo.

These were two great summers exploring the beaches and mountains of Kerry.

I noticed in the shop that the saddest and most depressing customers were those who bought religious periodicals. The shop used to be a Catholic repository for all kinds of religious artefacts and Mike and I threw all the statues and scapulars out the door. We discovered that religious books sold far better when mixed in with secular books. A religious section on its own sold hardly any books. The biggest demand was for books on depression. They constantly had to be re-stocked.

Sometimes I helped with services on Sundays. In Castlemaine, Co Kerry, I had a unique experience. The congregation passed around a hat for me and gave me a generous honorarium. I have never forgotten those kind, generous and thoughtful people of Castlemaine.

It was in Co Kerry that I met Charlie Graystack, the Dean of Ardfert and rector of Kenmare. 'Look at those pews,' he said to me one day, 'hallowed for generations with shiny Protestant arses!' At a service when he was making the announcements my children were amused when Charlie's trousers fell down. When Charlie was a curate in Birr, daily Morning Prayer was said. After some days the rector asked Graystack to explain his absence. 'As you were there, rector, I didn't see much point in the two of us being there.'

Killarney was an exciting cosmopolitan town with throngs of visitors from all over the world. Many of the tourists would come into our shop early in the morning. Some of them were not enjoying their holidays and needed a kind word. One of the most beautiful people to enter the shop was a local retired priest. Each morning he came in to buy his newspaper, and always had a warm greeting of good morning.

Kerry is lovely in the summer but it rains all winter. It is also a long distance from the east coast. The summer of 1984 was coming to a close when I received a postcard from my friend Jim McAleese in Co Meath. It simply said, 'How about Castlepollard and Oldcastle Parish?' I didn't know where these places were so I got out a map in the shop and discovered them. There were six churches, which wasn't encouraging.

Mike lent me his car and Jean and I went up to Castlepollard to scout the area. The parish had a fine Georgian rectory. I was interested and met one of the parochial nominators who was on holiday in West Cork. Parochial nominators are members of a parish chosen to elect a new rector along with four diocesan nominators and the bishop – nine in all.

CHAPTER 17

'Just clean living, bishop, clean living'

The bishop of Meath and Kildare, Donald Caird, was a remote figure to me and I had never really known him. He had a sharp mind and incisive wit. Donald Caird was very much a traditionalist and I think that he was nervous of appointing me to a parish. Wise man! He was critical and dubious of the charismatic movement and was nervous when I was going to set up a retreat centre in his diocese some years previously. Caird asked me what I had most learnt on the open road. I told him that I believed that fruit was more important than gifts.

When a former bishop of Meath was asked what diocese he came from the bishop replied, 'the dead see'! Bishop Caird was known affectionately as 'Donald Duck' and stories about him are legion. There is the tale of the day he arrived home for lunch. His wife was out. He smelt stew on the Aga and ate it. Later he saw a note from his wife instructing him to feed the cat. The cat's dinner was on the Aga!

Greeting people coming out of Oldcastle church, he met an American major Harry Hesse who asked the bishop how he was feeling. 'Not too well, Major.' 'You know bishop I had that same disease myself,' Major Harry replied. 'What's the cure, Major?' 'Just clean living, bishop, clean living.'

Major Harry was an American marine who came to Ireland for the hunting. Another marine lived in the parish as well and he was curious to know if Harry had fought in the banana war of Nicaragua in 1929. I told him to step into my car and we'd go and ask Harry. 'Harry, did you fight in the banana war of 1929?' 'Hell I sure did,' he replied. Major Harry told me on arriving in Oldcastle that 'if I preached shit he would shout "horseshit!"'

I was appointed rector of Castlepollard and Oldcastle in 1984. Castlepollard is an old estate village about fifteen miles north of Mullingar, near Lake Derravaragh. The parish was a huge geographical area, spreading as far as Lough Sheelin in

County Cavan. The two main families in the area were the Pollards and the Pakenhams. The Pollards had long since gone, but writers Thomas and Valerie Pakenham still lived in Tullynally Castle. Tullynally Castle is the largest lived-in castle in Ireland and next door to the rectory. Here on Lake Derravargh the legend of the Children of Lir began.

On one particular Sunday there were Pollards in church from the United States and Australia. It was an amazing coincidence as neither were aware of the other. I brought them to see the family tomb in the neglected graveyard. The headstone with the family crest had been vandalised and they could look into the vault at the bones of their ancestors. It was very distressing for them.

It was jokingly said that Castlepollard only came to life when there was a funeral. The last rector had been a former British army officer, an artist and keen fisherman. To a visiting friend, he said that Church of Ireland clergy were country gentlemen with a vague interest in religion. My successor in Castlepollard has recently been sent to prison for sex abuse of a young boy. It is amazing that Roman Catholic priests get high media attention and Church of Ireland clergy never get press attention. This reversed the trend.

The midlands are well populated with the big houses and the Anglo Irish. A writer once wrote that the Anglo Irish spent their time in Ireland involved in 'strenuous leisure' – horse riding, fishing, hunting and travelling. Basically they socialised among themselves and lived off incomes from Lloyds. When Lloyds collapsed their cupboards were bare. When I arrived in the midlands there was a retired colonel, naval commander, a German countess and six lowly majors.

Major Brabazon, known as 'Fitz' was a great character. Outside the bank one day I told him that he looked well. A scowl appeared on his face. 'There are three ages of man,' Fitz said, 'Youth, middle age, and Gee you're looking great'! In his early nineties he despaired of becoming a grandfather. His only son and daughter-in-law turned up trumps before he died and produced two grandsons. Their other grandfather, Howard Temple of Magees of Donegal fame, was a charming gentleman. As a token of thanks for baptising his grandchildren he invited me up to Donegal to have a suit made of the finest cloth. He told me that he wanted me to know how much he appreciated what we clergy did in the country. While people often knock the clergy Howard Temple's thoughtfulness was a source of great encouragement to me.

Parish appointments in Meath diocese took place in Church House in Dublin according to a long tradition. On one occasion two nominators from the parish, Major Brabazon and Robert Holmes, a wealthy farmer, were driving home to Castlepollard. They had elected a new rector that day. 'Do you know what we've done today, Robert?' Fitz asked. 'We've elected the man that will put us down!' That new rector did not bury either of them. One day near his end I drove Fitz down to the new graveyard so that he could pick out a plot. There I buried him some time later. When Fitz became housebound I brought him communion once a month. We always finished up with a glass of Jameson's whiskey. When I visited Major Harry Hesse I always got Jack Daniels bourbon. I had developed a taste for it when living in the United States. When the American major left Ireland to return to Maryland he left instructions that I was to get any bourbon on the premises. Harry Hesse did not live long after his return to the US. He was a traditionalist who liked the old English of the 1662 prayer book. He refused to use any new book and followed the services in the old book.

A grave experience

We needed a new graveyard as the old burial ground was abandoned. The flat site behind the church was ideal and some of the farmers helped me to restore the plot of ground. A retired stonemason did a lovely job repairing the stonewalls. At the first funeral a neighbour next door objected but I had done my homework. Ecclesiastical property was not then subject to local planning laws. The ground had already been passed as suitable by the Health Officer. When the matter was raised at the Westmeath County Council the Chairman, Senator Donie Cassidy stated that Norman Ruddock could build a hotel on the site if he wanted to. The prickly lady who objected was ironically enough a parishioner, and she herself was buried in the burial ground years later.

When I asked an Anglo Irish gentleman why Castlepollard and Oldcastle did not mix more, he told me they belonged to different hunts. A castle Catholic married to an Anglo Irish parishioner always came to church. She never took communion. When I asked her why she did not go to the local Catholic Church she said that she could not worship with the peasants.

A humbler resident was the local cobbler in Oldcastle, Sammy Lowdnes. He had a faded old sign in his workshop 'If you think you have problems wear tight shoes.' At the time of his funeral the parish priest, Father Eugene Conlan, said of Sammy, 'His voice was not heard in the marketplace.'

One of the monthly chores was to write notes for the diocesan magazine. To liven up the magazine some of us resorted to humour. One January the rector of Maynooth wrote that he had brought his wife breakfast in bed on New Year's Day. In the following issue I asked him if he had brought his wife a roll in bed with honey. The rector of Clane, a doctoral historian, Dr Adrian Empey and now principal of the Theological College entered the lists in the following edition. He wrote that a Lenten breakfast was a roll in bed without honey. An Anglo Irish straight laced lady reproached me for writing copy so close to the bone.

One strange incident was the request I received from a colleague to park a hearse with remains, in our rectory grounds. It was a pit stop on a long journey. It was strange seeing the hearse driving out the gate. How often do you see a hearse leaving a rectory? Was the rector dead? The hearse had travelled from County Down to a funeral in County Longford. It was very amusing.

CHAPTER 18

Ministry or Masonry

When Walton Empey came as new bishop of Meath and Kildare, he came to inject new life. Walton and I had been classmates in college. A decision was taken to close a large number of churches, surplus to need. Tribal warfare broke out. Four of the six churches in my parish were to close. Mountnugent issued a writ taking the bishop to court for denial of freedom to worship. The case did not go to court and the church was allowed to stay open once a month. Three other churches closed without much fuss. In one case all the furniture out of Loughcrew church was taken out and placed in Oldcastle church.

The reality of re-organisation was that there were now two churches open at either ends of the parish, sufficient for the needs of the people. One of the greatest problems is the disposal of furnishings. On one occasion I gave a parishioner a gift of Kilkenny marble. I had it valued at £200. It was a gift to pour oil on troubled waters over the closure of the local church. Some years later by accident I saw the font in that man's garden with a brass place attached stating that the font had been rescued from the rape of the church. I had given a parishioner the font for £5 as all his children had been baptised in it. Technically, fonts should be destroyed when no longer needed, as with altars. You can't win.

On another occasion an Anglo Irish family had no interest in salvaging the memorial with the names of all their ancestors. Their only interest was to take the surrounding marble for sale to an antique dealer as it was valuable and they left the family memorial lying in the grass.

The Squinting Windows

Bishop Walton arrived one morning to deconsecrate Drumcree church, near Delvin of the squinting windows. When we arrived the gates had been padlocked with a new padlock. The bishop had taken a lot of flack over church closures and was quite nervous that morning. He was shaking. He decided to take the deconsecration prayers in his car. Later I learnt that the local squire, a total eccentric, was hiding behind the church wall accompanied by a 'west Brit matriarch'. The decision to rationalise the number of churches in Meath and Kildare was a very courageous decision and Bishop Walton did not shirk his responsibilities.

Down the road at Collinstown there was a fear that the church there was about to be demolished. In the vault under the church lay the leaded coffins of the landed gentry. Their descendents arrived early one morning, and without any permission, proceeded to drag the leaded coffins down the steps and transport them away. There were words with local Germans who now lived in the big house and World War Two was about to be re-enacted. The local Garda phoned me and when I arrived the lead coffins were gone. Had they taken coffins to sell the lead, or had the coffins been re-interred? Some miles away there was an old cemetery and a local told me that he saw the coffins being dragged across the grass. Some time later the saga was reported in *Phoenix* magazine. There was never a word of apology for this dreadful conduct which was totally illegal. I had asked John Mulcahy of the *Phoenix* magazine if he knew where they got the story, but he had no recollection of it.

Barbeville was the seat of the Lyster Smythes at Collinstown. Palemona Lyster-Smythe was the last of the family and was married to the relation of a large Norwegian brewery owner. Palemona spent her time cruising up and down the Mediterranean. She ended her days in a nursing home in Nice which overlooked a crematorium. A memorial tablet was unveiled in her memory in Drumcree Church, now closed. The brewer from Norway arrived plus some of the Guinness relatives. After the service, we retired to the local pub. Many of the Anglo Irish ordered sherry, a drink now gone out of fashion. The publican had never served or been asked for sherry before and poured out tumblers of sherry. It was high comedy.

Barbaville had been bought by Franz Pohl, a German industrialist. He was a fascinating man. In Germany he told me that after the war he saw all the unemployed soldiers. He opened a factory for them, making car parts. When he came to Ireland he saw all the unemployed in the Midlands and started a factory for them at his home in Collinstown. He employed men and women and there was no retirement age. Pohl knew all the families and knew their backgrounds and their children. He told the bank manager in the Ulster Bank that he would support my church, if he thought that I was any good or worth supporting.

Franz Pohl's factory made car parts for Datsun cars and he also manufactured logos for the infamous De Lorean cars. He was paid! The factory also produced the aluminium strips and flashing for cars. The factory still works away.

The Lyster Smythes were not popular landlords. An IRA sympathiser, who did work for me, told me that his grand uncle was one of the party who shot the Lyster Smythes coming home from Collinstown Church. They meant to shoot the husband, but killed the wife by mistake. She was one of those who were in the lead coffins, dragged down the church steps.

The sexy squire and the rector's wife
One of the strangest incidents in the Midlands was the disappearance of the church minute book. Church records are carefully supervised and checked each year, as is all the silver and precious artefacts. Not long before an old man's death, he told me the story. The local squire was having an affair with the rector's wife. On one occasion the rector's wife set off by train to London with her lover. As rector's wife and president of the Mothers Union (a church women's group) this would not do. A courier was sent to drag her home. It was alleged that the rector had had an accident of a personal nature in the First World War, and was impotent. When the rector's wife was packing up and leaving the rectory, she noticed the church minute book. As she leafed through it she read of her adulterous affair with the squire. She lit a bonfire and burned the precious records. The squire owned the rectory and when he died he gave the rector's wife a gift of the house for services rendered.

Later on during my time there a wealthy American widow, Jean Welch, gave a present of the same house to friends. Jean Welch was married to an American mining millionaire; during my time there I took his funeral. He had died while wintering in

Florida. He was a friendly man but a hopeless alcoholic. Before Welch, Jean was married to one of the Bird's Custard family. She was well off. By this time a ballroom had been added to the house. In the space of fifty years a fine house and lands had been given twice as a gift.

Another strange story was that of Archbishop James McCann who had been a curate in Oldcastle. He rode a tall bicycle and dressed disastrously. The rector, Canon Kevin, who was there for over forty years was a dapper man, the very opposite, who drove a fast up-market motorcar. Archbishop McCann ended up in Armagh where he did not enjoy a happy time. When in hospital, he stated that he did not wish to be visited by the Church of Ireland Chaplain, who was a friend of mine. It is alleged that he never attended church again after his retirement, except for one funeral. What happened to the man who was a brilliant preacher? We will never know. Canon Kevin strangely enough had a private funeral and the only parishioners there were the churchwardens.

One of the interesting incidents was being called to Drumcree to make a will for the postmistress who was ill in bed. She died shortly afterwards and her relatives contested the will. I had to make an oath that she was of sound mind when she made the will. She didn't have much to leave. As I left the bedside of her thatched house she pulled out a twenty-pound note from under her pillow and thanked me for my help. That is the only will that I ever executed. I never knew why she asked the Church of Ireland Rector to act for her. Maybe she felt it would give her a greater degree of confidentiality.

The Wild West
Dessie O'Hare, known as 'the Fox' livened up Castlepollard one day. He arrived in town to rob two banks. The manager in the Ulster Bank nearly got a heart attack. Coming out of the Ulster Bank 'the Fox' shot at a garda. He missed him by a few inches and the bullet mark is still in the wall. Entering the Bank of Ireland he fired a bullet into the ceiling. The bank manager was upstairs in bed and the bullet missed his bed close by. 'The Fox' was later arrested at a garda roadblock in Co Tipperary. Castlepollard had experienced terrorism.

It was in Tullynally Castle, Castlepollard, Co Westmeath, that I founded the Derravagh Music Association in 1987. A committee was formed with the encouragement and enthusiasm of Thomas and Valerie Pakenham. The vision was to present only the very best of Irish and foreign artists. With the co-operation of my musical promoter brother John, our first concert featured the Franz Schubert string quartet from Vienna. A stage was bought and chairs. We continued to run four to five concerts each season, and I am delighted that the music continues to thrive. The concerts also brought new life to the castle, and became great social events which pollinated the community.

Through my wife's attendance at Maynooth University I came to know her lecturer, Liam McCarthy, a very professional and gifted counsellor. He came down to us in Co Westmeath to lead several seminars. He was also an excellent help to friends with marriage problems. Liam felt that I was not very stretched in the midlands and felt that I needed a work with greater challenge. That was to take place sooner than I realised. I called to mind what my American friend Joe said to me years ago at another career moment: 'You can't change the direction of a mule that's lying down.' I had spent nine years in the midlands, but it seemed time to face a new challenge.

CHAPTER 19

Aotearoa – Land of the Long Passing Cloud

New Zealand came to the notice of the world when Captain Cook landed in the Bay of Plenty on the east coast of the North Island. Many would-be settlers came from Australia to seek their fortune in the gold mines of the western shore of the South Island. However, the heavy forests deterred them, and over half of them returned across the Tasman Sea to Australia. Anglican missionaries arrived from Australia in the early days of the 19th century and set up a community at Keri Keri in the Bay of Islands in the north of the North Island. Some of the stone houses that they built are still standing. In the hills above the gold mines in the west coast, there are graveyards with headstones commemorating Irish settlers. When the Pakeha (white settlers) arrived there were already Maoris living in New Zealand. Some believed that the Maoris came from Alaska, and that they sailed across the Pacific Ocean to New Zealand.

From Wexford to Waimate
Two events drew me to think of New Zealand. My daughter Julie was living there and a tablet on the wall of Killurin Church in Co Wexford was erected in memory of Lieutenant Edward Beatty who had died in Waimate North, New Zealand, during the first Maori War of 1845

Edward Beatty left for New Zealand with a British Regiment between 1840 and 1844. This journey would have taken three months. The Maoris, under their leader Hone Heke, resolved to drive the British out of New Zealand. Four times, Hone Heke cut down the flagpole with the Union Jack at Russell in the Bay of Islands on the North Island. Heke wrote to the Governor, Captain W. Hobson, an Irishman, 'We will die for our country that God has given us!' Colonel Despard, the leader of the British regiment was a hopeless soldier, and the Maoris were victorious at the battle at Waimate.

Edward Beatty died in battle and he is buried in the grave-yard of the local Anglican church. It was a very moving experience for me to see the grave of an Irish soldier who had travelled from Wexford to New Zealand. It was also moving to stand beside the flagpole that the Maori Chief had cut down, and gaze out across the Pacific at the innumerable islands of the Bay of Islands.

In 1992, my daughter Julie, a mathematical geographer, emigrated to New Zealand with her husband Larry. They had met in Trinity College, Dublin. Larry was the first boy to go to university from his road in West Cabra. He went on to obtain a PhD at Trinity, and he presently is a professor of property at Auckland University, New Zealand. Julie spends her time at home schooling her four children. As public school classes are overcrowded, and as many of the children come from the islands, they arrive with no English. Home schooling is allowed by the New Zealand government, inspectors call periodically to examine standards, and there are state grants for books. All the home school families meet regularly for swimming, art, languages, ballet and for outings. When my grandchildren were assessed, they were two years ahead of children in state schools.

I went on some of their outings – one to an ice cream factory which was very popular. A fascinating outing was to the Waitakere Forest, outside Auckland. The children had to wear clothes of the early 19th century, and were not allowed sweets, cameras or mobile phones. They brought flour, butter, tea and milk to make griddle scones. Along the way they met actors, acting out early 19th century life. When the children reached a clearing, they were shown how to make a fire, make scones and how to make tea. Then they were shown how timber beams were pulled through the forest in the early 19th century.

The nineties were the years of long haul travel, thanks to our son, working in Thailand, who financed our trips. One year we travelled from London to Thailand, and from there to New Zealand. From New Zealand we flew to Japan where our daughter Karen was studying Japanese. The final leg of the journey was across the Arctic Circle to London. In Japan Karen met her future husband, Jonathan, a Jewish student from Israel, studying Japanese.

My son's wife Janphen is Thai, and a wonderful cook. They have arrived in Ireland to open a new business, along with their three children. Karen has arrived back in Ireland to lecture in Japanese at Trinity College, while her husband Jonathan is developing a translation business.

Kyoto was a fascinating city which reminded us of an ancient civilisation. It is extremely difficult to find your way around Japan with no Japanese. One Christian writer, Shusaku Endo, wrote exciting novels, focusing on the persecution of Christians in the southern island of Kyushu. The Portuguese Jesuits came to Japan in the 17th century from Portuguese Macau, and risked arrest and torture. Many of them were put standing in hot springs of intense heat, or tied to crucifixes as the tide came in. Some of the Jesuits gave in, and betrayed their brother priests. The Japanese were militantly anti-Christian, and it was only in the 19th century that an American boat ran the gauntlet and arrived in Edo, as Tokyo was then known. These were the first foreigners to arrive in Japan: the renowned Jesuits who renounced their faith were known as apostates, and lived out their lives in Japan in disgrace.

A fascinating story concerns our daughter Lynn, then a primary school teacher in Dublin. She decided to take a holiday to visit her sister Karen who was then teaching in a church school in Uganda. We had not heard of her for weeks, and we were concerned for her safety in a disturbed and restless country. One morning, as I drove down the Stillorgan Road in Dublin, I saw a nun standing at a bus stop. I felt moved to stop and give her a lift. When she got into the car she said: 'You're Karen Ruddock's father, and her sister has arrived in Uganda. I saw Karen last week on my way home from Uganda!' If ever I experienced a miracle of the grace of God this was it. I believe that this incident was one of the most moving of my life.

One amusing incident in New Zealand took place when I visited friends of my daughter. The host had been an Anglican layreader, had become disenchanted with Anglicanism, and was now part of a house church with my daughter and son-in-law's family. The host, knowing I was some kind of clergyman, was keen to find out what denomination I belonged to. Finally, he asked me 'if I frocked up on Sunday!'

The forests in the Northlands of New Zealand contain the massive Kauri trees. They are now a protected species, as too many have been cut down for building and furniture. There was an outcry in Auckland when it was decided to put a roof of Kauri wood in the new Anglican Cathedral. I sent Thomas Pakenham of tree fame a postcard of the largest Kauri tree in the world. He told me that my postcard had encouraged him to write his bestseller, *Remarkable Trees of the World*.

The Maritime Museum in Auckland has boats of every kind that are used in the Pacific. It also has registers of all the passengers who arrived by boat in New Zealand in the early days of the 19th century. Many of the boats were Irish. When they arrived in New Zealand people often had to stay on board for months, as there was no accommodation for them. Many died of seasickness on the long journey, which now takes only twenty-five hours by jet.

CHAPTER 20

A Life Threatening Disease

The memory of that visit to the local doctor on a quiet Sunday evening still lives with me. I've held back from putting down on paper my reflections on a serious illness – I believed that the passage of time would give me a greater degree of objectivity. A doctor friend encouraged me to describe the experience in order to help others. It's such a personal trauma that I wonder if I can describe it clinically. I have always focused on health and swept aside the negativity of disease. One more wounded healer may bring comfort to another in charting the reality of cancer.

'I Feel Very Frightened'

I had felt that something was wrong for weeks. Suddenly the disease erupted like a volcano. The local doctor felt it was serious – he said that he hadn't come across the same symptoms for over a year. He advised me to pack my bag and get ready for hospital. As I drove home to the rectory I was devastated – loved ones were shattered. We don't give much thought to our mortality in the midst of good health. I asked my wife Jean how she felt and she replied, 'I feel very frightened.' A very loving, generous and devoted daughter Lynn wept. Cancer is always knocking at someone else's door – never at ours. It isn't happening – it astounds me – it's unbelievable.

'Relief?'

My friend the local surgeon, Peter Magill, phoned me. He told me not to worry. A course of antibiotics caused the lump to decrease to apparent normality. The surgeon was pleased – all would be well. Going out the door of his office for the last time he stopped me and as a final check he sent me up for a sonar scan. The prognoses was serious. Surgery was called for. The biopsy indicated a seminoma. A doctor friend in Co Wexford felt that this was generally a disease of young men. Seminomas weren't too serious. My surgeon arranged for me to see Doctor Desmond Carney at the Mater Hospital – he told me that Dr Carney was the best oncologist in the land. I will always be grateful that I was referred to such a dynamic man. He is a fine looking person who radiates positive energy. He also has had the advantage of clinical experience in the United States. He was honest and open and he 'shoots from the hip'.

He told me that further tests indicated that I had a high grade lymphoma – a 'horse of a different colour'. It seemed like a death sentence. I wept. He advised me to ring my bishop immediately and to obtain a leave of absence. While I was officially on sick duty, I was still able to do my work in Wexford. I was only off duty for two Sundays, and struggled through it – nausea, tiredness and all. The sooner I got into hospital, the sooner treatment would begin. He encouraged me by saying that non-Hodgkins lymphomas have a high recovery rate. A nephew had had the same disease. The treatment would take five months and I would have to drop all engagements. Dr Carney explained the side effects and assured me that no expense would be spared to make me well again.

Trying to Cope

As I drove home to Wexford to my new parish I was paralysed emotionally – I don't know how I drove the car – I was in bits. I had been instituted rector by my bishop only four days after major surgery. I was as weak as a kitten as I tried to disguise the reality of my illness. That night I had my first parish meeting of young parents. I don't know how I got through it. On the Sunday I tried to convey to my people that I had cancer. From that moment until the end of my treatment they upheld me and sustained me in their prayers. I believe that the more we share our feelings the more it encourages others to share their feelings and empathise with one another. 'Jesus wept' – there is a poverty of confessional preaching from our pulpits. We speak about healing but are slow to reveal our own nakedness. From that day on countless people around the world were praying for me.

Here I was, sent to an exciting new field of ministry in Wexford and almost immediately I was being sent into exile after only arriving. It was cruel, unjust, unfair, merciless. I shuddered – was my work finished?

A Different Life

Leaving home and loved ones for hospital is an emotional upheaval – especially when the hospital is far from home. Even leaving my adorable cat 'Puddy' tears me apart. It reminded me of my first trip to boarding school in the hungry forties. Getting into pyjamas is even strange and humbling. The staff might as well have stamped a serial number on the pocket. Why does everyone in hospital have to wear pyjamas or nightgowns? I made it a habit to get dressed at 7 o'clock each morning. One lady doctor who attended me said that if she ran a hospital she would have all the patients dressed. I'm not in the habit of wearing pyjamas – I find it much more comfortable and liberating to sleep naked. But sharing a ward with three strangers is in itself a challenge. An oncology nurse was assigned to look after me – she was a real professional, nurse Aine Kelly. I'm sure I exasperated her many times, but she never gave up on me – almost never. I owe her a great debt of gratitude.

I asked a consultant to explain to me what lymphomas were – he sat down on my bed and told me. Basically it is cancer of the lymph glands. The barrister across the ward with the same disease shocked and rocked me. 'Don't ask questions,' he said, 'The less you know the better.' It wasn't very encouraging and it unsettled me. This was a moment when I longed for a private room. I was so innocent and ignorant that I did not know what chemotherapy was. I assumed that it was some kind of radiation treatment. I resolved that I didn't want to hear or listen to any more negativity. I would look to the light.

The Daily Round

Countless blood tests, x-rays, cat scans, piles of steroids, and other medication became the daily round. Temperature taking had a bearing on 'parole'. Painful lumbar punctures still haunt me. Low blood counts, septicaemia, hair loss, and possible sterility were facts of the strange new journey. Sterility for younger people is a real problem. Losing one's beard gives one a new anonymity and *persona*. Friends don't recognise you in the street. Beardless, a gentle bishop's wife tells me that it's not me! The wonder drug Neupogen raises the blood count – one hundred and fifty euro a fix. Blood transfusions filled me with a new lease of life. An injection of someone else's energy. While in hospital I read tennis star Arthur Ashe's autobiography. For him blood tests went horribly wrong – he received blood shortly before it was tested for the aids virus. He was given contaminated blood.

A Sense of Humour

A Roman Catholic periodical asked me to write an article on Lenten preparation in the midst of my illness. I laughed. I offered to write an article on my present situation but it received no response. Another editor looking for an article wasn't interested in an article on cancer. When I entered a room on occasions there was an embarrassed silence. When I left the room my wife Jean would be asked 'how is he?' Even relatives found it difficult to discuss the subject. The big 'C' (what dreadful terminology) seems to be a convenient way not to mention the illness. People I found were confused with my cancer, and they are further confused if you recover. My treatment under Dr Carney cost thousands of pounds and what would one do without Voluntary Health Insurance. I would encourage those who do not have medical insurance to take it out. I know of no greater priority. My ever thoughtful and kind Bishop Noel found generous grants for expenses.

Getting out of hospital after treatment – especially after a time of painful infection – has few equals. However the consultant did allow me out to eat in the evenings. I avoided nausea most of the time when fasting. Nausea tablets are most effective. I developed a strategy of asking about going home three or four days before I knew that I would be released. The consultant never kept me a day longer than was necessary.

I've never dwelt on illness and I've always been exasperated at healing prayer meetings where the whole focus is on illness. It was always debilitating. Jesus sees us whole. In an American hospital last year I saw a beautiful sensitive young woman who recently tried to commit suicide – it was a close call. Cal (not her real name) was in a North Carolina hospital. A family friend asked me to visit her when I was on a visit to the United States.

Cal told me the horrific story of how she had been sexually abused by her father and brother over a period of years. It is a miracle she survived. Ministering to Cal was one of the most rewarding pastoral experiences of my life. I contemplated how I fought to hold on to life while others try to end it all. Life is a precious gift ...

I've tried to describe clinically my walk with cancer – before the perceptions fade from my memory. So far my regular check-ups give me confidence. And what has my illness taught me? I have resolved to spend the rest of my ministry focused on people and to sidetrack money, meetings, and things. I have resolved to do what is important – not urgent. I feel that as hospital chaplain I have a fresh empathy for those suffering from cancer. I hope that I can encourage people to share their feelings about it.

I was humbled by the countless people who called to see me. My wife Jean's perpetual attention never wavered – some forget the strain on the loved one nearby. I have experienced the joys of family life 'in sickness and in health' – 'to love and to cherish till death us do part'. It's the bedrock of society. There's a new journey to be walked – time is precious. It's ironic that a life threatening disease should open new doors of understanding. I have met special people in an exciting life which has taken me over the world, but no group more special than Dr Carney and his oncology staff at St Benedict's Ward at the Mater. Cancer isn't always a death sentence – great strides are being made, thanks to selfless people. The battle against cancer is unceasing. I decided to wage war on cancer – I was dying to live.

Non-Hodgkins Cancer
Non-Hodgkins is cancer of the lymph glands, and is not uncommon among young men. The disease is also more prevalent today than in times past – women also contract this type of cancer. If one is to get cancer, this is the one to have, as it is very treatable with a high success rate of recovery. A few years ago while doing my rounds in hospital as chaplain, I came across a widow in bed. She told me that her husband had died of Non-Hodgkins in the 1970s, but that there was then no treatment for his disease. He simply died. He would probably be alive today if he got the disease.

The Padlocked Church

In the spring of 1993 I received a phone call from George Rothwell in Wexford. The parish was now vacant and he wondered if I would be interested in a move. George was a parochial nominator, one of the parish lay people appointed to seek a new rector. I always had a great love for Wexford and longed to be near the sea. I asked George to put my name in the hat and I waited anxiously for an interview. At interview I noticed that no woman was present, and all the nominators were old men. Except for George Rothwell, none of them seemed to have any vision for the parish. We had built a retirement home in Wexford several years previously, and as I walked down the main street I noticed that Saint Iberius Church was always closed and padlocked. I said to the Lord: 'Lord, why do you allow this church to be padlocked?' Little did I realise that a year later, the Lord answered my prayer and sent me to Wexford.

It was to be the beginning of eleven years of a wonderful, satisfying and exciting ministry. I only wish that I could have had a longer ministry in Wexford at a younger age. Maybe the time was not right. I was delighted when my old friend, Bishop Noel Willoughby phoned me to tell me of my appointment. For me it was a real homecoming.

Au Revoir

My farewell function was held in Tullynally Castle. The parishioners had put on a special evening with Percy French music and the singer, John Roche, was a native of Wexford. I was delighted that the evening was taking place at the castle, because we had enjoyed so many special evenings there. Thomas and Valerie Pakenham were so generous, opening their home to the community.

It was a coincidence that the BBC were filming a feature at the castle that day. They decided to stay and film the rector's departure. The main hall was crowded and I received many tokens of gratitude. My friend and classmate, Bishop Walton Empey was also present that night. It was a community evening with all creeds and classes present which warmed my heart.

The Sunny South East

'The sunny south east' is a tourist promotion that has stuck. However, it is a sunny paradise. I was weak as a kitten when I arrived in Wexford for my institution service. I had only come out of hospital after surgery a few days before. A Church of Ireland service of institution of a rector is a special event in the life of the community. The mayor of Wexford and the members of the Corporation were present that evening. In his sermon Bishop Noel Willoughby reminded the congregation of the day we played cricket in Carlow. Noel Willoughby was not a cricketer, but when he arrived to watch a match at Carlow, we were a player short and Noel came in as 11th man. I told Noel: 'You block, and I'll hit off the runs.' Noel blocked splendidly, I kept the bowling, and the runs were hit off. 'Bishops are blockers' he said to great laughter in the church. Physically I don't know how I survived that evening, but I did. George Rothwell, welcoming me to the parish, said 'There was a man sent from God, and his name was Norman.'

During interviews George Rothwell had casually remarked that he had lumps under his armpits, and that he was going to see a doctor next day. He too had cancer, Non-Hodgkins. That was the first time that I had heard the name, and ironically enough I had the same disease a few months later. George struggled with his illness which he bore with great courage, but he lost the fight. I felt his loss greatly, for George loved the Lord, and still had so much to contribute to his church. At times I felt guilty that I had recovered and he had not.

CHAPTER 21

'It's About Pyjamas'

On my journey to The Mater Private Hospital I called in to a supermarket to buy a dressing gown and from there went straight to Saint Benedict's ward on the top floor of the Mater Private Hospital. I jokingly called it 'death row' and I resolved that night that I would fight the bastard cancer. I was in bits that evening as I changed into my boxer shorts and was assigned my bed in a four bedded ward. It is interesting that the cancer ward is generally on the top floor of a hospital and the morgue is tucked away in the basement, away from everyone.

During the first few days the most upsetting feature was to see so many people with no hair and white faces. Chemotherapy commenced for me several days later after a multitude of blood tests and x-rays. I found it startling when my hair began to fall out until eventually it was all gone.

I came to know many fine fellow travellers in hospital. Big Jim McStay who had been in the petrol business was in the bed beside me. He was a great encourager and lifted my spirits when I was down. He was a fine handsome man. Fr Michael Ryan, parish priest of Carrick-on-Shannon was also in the same ward and he too had Non-Hodgkins. He bore his illness with great patience. We had known each other years before when we served on the National Charismatic Council. The third companion on our ward was Frank Jackson from Wexford. He found it difficult acclimatising himself to hospital life. I came to know Frank's wife Imelda and beautiful daughter years later in Wexford. None of my ward companions survived the illness, and I often wondered why I had a reprieve.

I discovered that I knew others on our landing. Mary Earl from Virginia had been a member of the same golf club. She actually won a competition between treatments. Mary died while I was in hospital. Her lovely husband Joe who also played golf never failed to call and say hello. Peggy McCabe from Mount

Nugent used to come to our concerts in Tullynally Castle and loved traditional jazz. I discovered Peggy by accident as she heard my voice in the corridor and shouted, 'That's Norman Ruddock!'

I found that if I did not eat I could cope with chemotherapy. I associated hospital food with the treatment and could not eat it. Thankfully I was allowed out at night to eat and many friends entertained me. My veins were too weak and I was asked to have an intraport put into my chest. It basically acts like a petrol pump, pumping blood transfusions and chemotherapy into my body. This required surgery. I don't know what happened but I developed septicaemia afterwards. This blood poisoning in conjunction with a low blood count called for large doses of antibiotics in liquid form. At this point I could hardly breathe and I felt that I was dying. Mercifully I pulled through.

After periods of treatment I was allowed home. Seeing the sight of Wexford across the bridge was an unbelievably wonderful experience. After about a week my blood count would fall very low and I generally got an infection as I had no resistance. This meant immediate return to the Mater and these periods of treatment were hard to bear. One lumbar puncture stands out in my memory as the pain was excruciating. Luckily the next time I was undergoing surgery I did not feel the lumber puncture.

The nurses were all highly trained and efficient. I must have been the most difficult patient in the hospital, but I was dying to live. I would begin asking Desmond Carney the consultant if I could go home on the morrow. I felt that if I kept asking I would be released. A high temperature cancelled out freedom to leave. I waited all day for a heart surgeon to check me out. I resolved to get the evening train to Wexford and I told the nurses that my time was as important as the consultant's. He was annoyed that I did not wait.

The ever efficient Desmond Carney always did his rounds early in the morning. He is an intensely fit man, still playing squash, and coping professionally with negativity and life threatening diseases every day. My funniest experience in hospital was when he asked to see me privately. 'It's about pyjamas,' he said. 'There have been complaints that you don't wear pyjamas. This is a Catholic hospital and they are very prim and proper.' Actually the consultant said that he didn't wear pyjamas either! I often intended to send him silk pyjamas from Thailand or Singapore.

Desmond Carney kindly gave up precious time to give a lecture on cancer in St Iberius Church, Wexford, on several occasions. He told the touching emotional story of how his niece wrote to her father saying that her one wish for Christmas was that daddy would give up smoking. Her father, Desmond Carney's brother-in-law, contracted lung cancer in his early forties. He confessed that it was no one's fault but his own. I often wonder if I would have contracted cancer had I never smoked.

One other story deserves re-telling. An over-pietistic priest entered our ward selling religious cards. He told us that we were born to suffer. I wanted to shout 'Bullshit' but in deference to my Catholic fellow patients I said nothing. I found it incredible that this priest had carte blanche permission to visit wards and spread such negativity. We were born to celebrate and enjoy life, to walk in the resurrection garden of new life and not to remain at Calvary. Here I must pay tribute to the faithfulness and cheerfulness of the Roman Catholic chaplain in the hospital who always had a kind word.

Cancer has taught me the value of time. I have discovered in a new way that each day is important. I will never forget the loving kindness of my schoolteacher daughter Lynn who dropped in to see me each day after school. She cycled everyday from Blackrock to Castleknock School, yet never forgot me. One night I awoke in bed and there before me was what I thought a dream. My daughter Karen had flown in from Japan to see me. My son Norman arrived from England and was in hospital at 8 am to see my oncologist. I never loved my children as much as at that time. Daughter Julie in New Zealand, who I know prayed for me constantly, sent me a beautiful embroidered poem by Charles Wesley.

Away my needless fears
And doubts no longer mine
A ray of heavenly light appears
A messenger divine

Thrice comfortable hope
That calms my troubled breast
My Father's hand prepares the cup
And what he wills is best

He knows whate'er I want
He sees my helplessness
And always readier is to grant
That I to ask his grace

My fearful heart he reads
Secures my soul from harms
And underneath his mercy spreads
Its everlasting arms

Many friends called. One touching visit was that of Kerry Waterstone, former rector of Tullamore. He pulled out an old 1662 *Book of Common Prayer* and prayed with me. He had prepared me for confirmation at Kilkenny College. At boarding school in Galway Grammar he was nicknamed *Uisce Cluiche* – Water Stone! He now lives in a redundant church converted into a pleasant house, near Tullamore. His house is surrounded by graves which remind one of our mortality. He took early retirement in protest against the ordination of women.

At my lowest ebb I felt that I could not carry on any longer. I had a surprise visit from a priest friend, Neal Carlin, from Donegal. There he runs a centre for ex-prisoners and alcoholics, near the Donegal/Derry border. Neal laid hands on me and I felt a great sense of inner peace, and I began to improve.

CHAPTER 22

Opening the Doors

My first task in Wexford was to arrange for the opening of St Iberius Church each day. The local people had never seen the magnificent interior, until the Franciscans used the church temporarily for Mass while the Friary was being restored. The Wexford Festival chief executive Jerome Hynes asked permission to use St Iberius Church for lunchtime concerts. This provided tremendous exposure for the church. This arrangement has continued successfully over the last eleven years. The annual festival service in the church took on a new lease of life with the corporation and mayor present each year. The worship at the service was truly uplifting with one of the bishops of the Church of Ireland generally preaching each year.

During the opera festival another innovation was the art exhibitions, with some artists more successful than others. Several months after I arrived I was approached by two keen music enthusiasts. They had a vision to form Music for Wexford and to bring chamber music to Wexford. Music for Wexford soon became firmly established with most of its concerts taking place in St Iberius Church. Thanks to an Arts Council grant we were able to bring international artists to Wexford. Another innovation was music in the workplace with lunchtime concerts in venues such as the Environmental Protection Agency, the county library and the Heritage Centre. During a summer series each year young Irish artists were invited to perform. Some went on to international careers, such as Finghin Collins and Robin Tritchler. One wonderful weekend we had the celebrated composer John Rutter for an all day choral workshop. His eighteen-year-old son, a university student, had been killed crossing the street in Cambridge. John came to us on the anniversary of his son's death, which was generous indeed. Interestingly enough, John Rutter had attended the same school in North London as another famous composer, John Taverner. Other independent promotions included the Sonare eighty piece orchestra from the US, and a wonderful Cossack choir from the Ukraine. Their Irish tour had been badly promoted and they had so little money that they stayed in the Vincent de Paul hostel in Wexford. Fortunately we had a full house for their concert. They were quite an outstanding choir. The Loch Garman Silver Band, the Wexford Male Voice Choir, and Ladies choir all used the church venue over the years. The Wexford School of Music also held their students' concerts in the church. Some would have said that the church was becoming a concert hall, but I saw the church as embracing all of life and not simply religious events. The church was gradually becoming a focus for all kinds of activity in the community. It was coming alive.

When I arrived in Wexford I had the care of three churches and in 1995 I had two more added to my 'parish' at Taghmon and Horetown. Henry Francis Lyte, author of 'Abide With Me' was once a curate at Taghmon.

In 2002 the parish of Rosslare was vacant, and it was decided not to make an appointment as there was not enough work for a priest. The parish was put under the charge of the rector of Wexford, who was to be assisted by a curate. This extra addition meant that there were now nine churches to be looked after. There seems to be no diocesan impetus to close churches; the *status quo* continues, and keeping the tribal shrines open seems to be all important. There are now 50% less clergy than when I started in Ferns diocese, but there are the same number of committees. Auxiliary priests and lay readers prop up a system long out of date.

I remember taking a service at Kilgarvan near Kenmare in Co Kerry when the only parishioners present were a clergy widow and her special needs son. The church had been an estate church of the Orpen family, but when the estate died, the congregation dried up. The church was in a dreadful state and bat dirt covered the altar and pews. When I asked the clergy widow why she did not worship in Kenmare she said that we must keep the flag flying. Too many people would express the same sentiments. The church is now used for other purposes, and has been beautifully restored.

'There are no pockets in a shroud'

The restoration of St Iberius church was completed in 1992 at a cost of over €500,000. This did not take into account the bank interest paid over the years. When I arrived the debt was €200,000. This undertaking was a great act of courage, but I don't believe that much pragmatism was exercised in wondering how the bill would be paid. I have always believed that God will provide and he did. Money isn't burned in a big pile. It is simply a question of moving it from one bulky pocket to another empty pocket in need. My first initiative was to start a stewardship or envelope scheme where people would pay weekly to the maintenance of the church. This scheme greatly improved finances. The Heritage Council had refused a grant because they maintained the original had not been restored. Some time later the Heritage Council changed its mind and made a substantial grant. Another wonderful benefactor was the late Peter Prentice SC, one of the finest and most courteous gentlemen I have ever met. He once wrote me a letter with a grant of five thousand pounds from a charity that he supervised. However the enclosed cheque read 25,000 pounds! When I rang Peter he told me that the cheque was right and the letter wrong. He was a fairy godfather over the years.

On another occasion I was invited to lunch at Tullynally Castle. Sitting beside me was a charming lady who happened to mention that she was godmother to a child of a very wealthy man. In fact I knew that he was chairman of a large charitable foundation in the United Kingdom, and his father had been a parishioner of mine. I asked the lady if she would mind if I mentioned her name to the businessman and she readily agreed. The foundation made a generous donation but their rules specified that the money could only be paid inside the UK. I wrote to the Archbishop of Armagh, Archbishop Eames, for help with a perfectly legal solution, cutting through much red tape. As Archbishop Eames had preached at the re-opening of St Iberius I thought that he would have been more helpful. Maybe he had an over cautious legal mind or thought that I was money laundering. Peter Prentice SC had advised me how to avail of the funds granted by the English foundation, and he was most helpful.

In a very quiet way the money was collected and the millennium was set as the date to have the debt paid off. We had a celebration dinner during the first week of the new millennium. The debt on the church was now wiped off in eight short years. I was delighted that Peter was able to come to the celebrations at the Ferrycarrig Hotel, Wexford, with his wife. I had just finished writing this chapter when I heard of Peter Prentice's death. He enriched the legal, commercial and charitable foundations in Ireland. To be in his company was a tonic.

The more we give the more we receive. When Horetown parish was added to Wexford there was now a surplus rectory. The people of Horetown very generously used the money from the rectory sale to restore and extend Wexford Union Rectory. Years late Horetown received €200,000 from the estate of Canon Fry who had been rector there for a short time in the early days of the century. His hobby was model railways. He had a model railway at Horetown, and you can see the Fry memorial railway at Malahide Castle, near Dublin. He was a bachelor who gave his housekeeper a life interest in his estate and she only died in the mid 1990s. Fry spent most of his ministry in Julianstown in Co Meath, and only four years in Horetown. It is a mystery why he was so generous to Horetown. The miracle is that Horetown people's generosity was richly rewarded. If you find a mean parish you will find mean people, and if you find a mean rectory you will find a mean rector. When I came to the Park Rectory in Wexford I found that all the window openings had been nailed firmly. This was a cheap way of dealing with draughts. This was a death-trap if there had been a fire. Now there is good double glazing and new windows.

I have never had any problem raising money. It is also true that when you give something away, it comes back with greater generosity. I have always had the rule to ask for funds only once. That also allows people the freedom to refuse. I was annoyed recently when I was asked for the ex-directory telephone number of a wealthy friend. It was a begging request and I declined to be used. How many would phone the wealthy to find out how their health was, or how they were keeping? These people are simply seen as purveyors of funds – people to be used.

In most parishes the local church is the tribal shrine, to be maintained at all costs. The church building is of far greater importance than a comfortable rectory for the rector. Try to close one of these tribal shrines, and you will raise a hornet's nest. Once I agreed to have a church restored. It cost many thousands. What the parishioners gave was negligible. It is assumed that central church funds will provide money, or the local community. It is true to say that the Church of Ireland seems to be the Catholic Church's favourite charity! Putting a roof on a church building is a greater priority than other needs. Masonry is more important than ministry. When I look at church accounts I always look to see how much the parish has given away the past year, and how many vocations have been fostered there.

Once when speaking to a ladies' group, I was discussing the ways money is raised for the church – jumble sales, second had clothes, hand-me-downs – the things that we are throwing out. At the end of the meeting the rector arrived, and announced a jumble sale. Everyone laughed. Guessing the weight of a cake or the number of smarties in a jar will raise precious little money. I would reckon that a hundred people could write a cheque for a thousand euro and wouldn't miss it. An instant hundred thousand euro. It can be done.

CHAPTER 23

Where were the Children?

Patrick Semple, whose father ran a jewellery business, wrote about his native Wexford in his book, *Believe it or not*. He wrote about the congregation that I inherited – a handful of elderly adults. Where were the young families? Where were the children? The first task was to involve the children in worship, and their parents too. A childrens' choir was formed from the children at the school, and over forty children enlisted. I was fortunate to obtain the services of a brilliant choirmaster and organist, Eanna McKenna, who did wonders with the children. The appointment of an old friend, Ivan Dungan as principal of Saint Iberius school cemented the relationship between church and school. Ivan had started life as a Christian Brother, and found his spiritual home in the Church of Ireland. A family communion service involved the children. We had congregations of up to 200 for family services. If it is to be a family communion then I believe all the family should partake. It was my custom to give all the children bread at communion, if parents gave their consent. Confirmation has failed, and is a passing out parade. As one bishop said jokingly, if you want to get rid of bats, confirm them and you'll never see them again.

It is not the custom of the Church of Ireland to give Holy Communion to children before Confirmation, which takes place generally between the age of eleven and fourteen. However, as young Roman Catholic children have already made their first communion at an early age, they come up for communion at the family service. The Church of Ireland has dragged its heels on this issue, and legislation to allow earlier communion has been defeated in General Synod several times. It is a ridiculous situation. If it is a family service, surely the whole family should participate. At least the children should receive the bread. My grandsons put out their hands and I joyfully give them the bread of life. If children are heavy into computers, play station games etc, then they are intelligent enough to know what Holy Communion is all about. The greatest cowboys, wife beaters and thieves can receive Holy Communion without any questions asked.

Dear Kenneth with a grin on his face put his hands up to receive the bread at Communion. I held back at the last moment from giving him the sacrament. I did not know either if his parents would approve. After the service he jokingly said to me, 'Ah, I nearly caught you out!' Some months earlier Kenneth told me how he had been at a Christian camp where he had decided to follow Jesus. He was so intense and earnest. Kenneth was my son Norman's best friend, and Kenneth died in a tree accident about a week after we left the parish. Looking back I am sorry that I did not give Kenneth the bread that day. Paul Lebeau, a Belgian theologian said at a Catholic conference that I attended, that the sacrament of Holy Communion is not definitive. Man cannot say who can receive and who cannot. That statement was a result of a Roman Catholic decision not to give Holy Communion to Christians of other traditions at a charismatic conference in Dublin.

My son attended Confirmation classes, and when I asked him if he wanted to be confirmed at the end of the course he said no. Years later, while we were visiting his friend Kenneth's grave, he told me that I must have wondered why he did not want to be confirmed. He told me that the clergyman would not answer his questions, but told him that he would answer the questions after the class. My son Norman felt that the cleric was not man enough to deal with the issues on the spot, and he lost respect for him. My son still grieves for his friend Kenneth, and visits his family.

In tandem with the shortage of candidates for the ministry, the ministry of the Church of Ireland has been augmented with women priests and candidates from the Roman Catholic Church. One Catholic bishop castigated a priest for changing to the Church of Ireland, and was very bitter indeed. Why do Roman priests leave the celibate ministry? For some it may be a desire to be married, but I believe it is more a rejection of power and authoritarianism. Clerical sex abuse has rocked the Catholic Church, not least in the Diocese of Ferns.

The conferring of the Freedom of Wexford on Bishop Noel Willoughby, the retiring Church of Ireland Bishop of Ferns was a historic event which took place in St Iberius Church. He had gone to school in the Tate School, now the municipal buildings, and had worshipped in St Iberius Church as a boy. I was delighted to see guests from north and south of the border, marching behind the local brass band as they played the Republican tune 'A Nation Once Again'. Notables present included the mayors of Kilkenny and Dublin, the Bishop of Ferns Brendan Comiskey, Archbishop Walton Empey of Dublin and Jean Kennedy Smith, US ambassador to Ireland. Jean is the sister of Wexford Freeman, the late President John F. Kennedy. The Kennedys hailed from Dunganstown, near New Ross.

Churches and congregations are often like besieged fortresses. The very fact that churches are padlocked all week says something. There are those inside the fortress who are card carrying paid up members of the tribe. Those outside the fortress are looked on as second class Christians or pagans. They don't contribute to the upkeep of the shrine, have little knowledge or interest in what goes on inside the fortress and little effort is made to bring them into the church community. When they do come to worship, generally no one speaks to them and they are considered visitors or strangers. The amusing story is told of the man who came to church and no one spoke to him. He then wore his hat into church and the churchwardens came and asked him to remove it. He told them he wore his hat to see if anyone would speak to him! On one occasion in a rural parish where I served, a large family of ex-Roman Catholics came to church. After the service a very pious member of the congregation asked why they didn't go to their own church. Are we reaching out at all? On another occasion a fortress lady wrote to all the young families castigating them for forsaking the fortress. She had driven them further away. One of the young mothers whose home I visited regularly showed me the bitter letter. 'If this is Christian, I want nothing to do with it,' she said. They now attend house church.

The fortress mentality and its weakness were dramatically revealed to me when I visited a nominal member of the parish in hospital. He was militantly anti-church and told me to get the hell out of the ward. As the weeks went by I never gave up on John (not his real name) and when his cancer worsened he became a very needy person indeed. John knew he was dying and wished to change his will for his relatives never came to see him in hospital. With his wife present, John asked me what to do with his considerable assets, for he had no ideas himself. He had left his wife an interest in his share of the estate, but he was planning for the future. I mentioned St Iberius Church, and he told me how he had a great love for the building even though he didn't patronise it. John decided to remember the church in his will, and to ask his solicitor to call. I thought that John would soon forget his decision, but when I returned from a New Zealand holiday he happily told me everything was arranged. He became a great lover of the sacrament during his last days, and John died very peacefully in my presence one day.

As John lay dying of leukaemia I told him the story of when I was in an intensive care ward in Belfast. I was very ill and felt I was dying. I felt that I was being carried over the great divide, and it was very beautiful. I did not want to come back. Since that experience I have not feared death. John died in my arms.

John still speaks to me of the host of beautiful people outside the fortress whose lives have not been touched, or reached. I believe that visiting is the heart of ministry, but computers, conferences, seminars and meetings keep clergy from the heart of the work.

In contrast to John, I had no success with George (not his real name). I could get no response when we met. When threatened, I asked him if he was worried about dying, suddenly he lifted his big stick and ran me! At least my effort to get a response was productive.

A new family had come to Wexford, and attended the church regularly. I also called on them at their new home several times. Then they stopped coming to church, and I failed to follow them up. One day I met one of the family, and asked him why they no longer attended the church. He told me that they felt outsiders. While all the other people spoke to each other, no one spoke to them. They were very much still Christians, but they had not felt a welcoming spirit. If I had known of the problem I could have dealt with it, but I had failed to notice their need of fellowship and companionship. On the other hand, they may have been looking for an excuse to bow out. I do not know, but it was a case of pastoral failure.

Ministry outside the fortress is so much more exciting and energising than 'the Urbs Fortitudinis', which means 'we have a strong city'. It should read 'we have a strong settee'. I believe that we as Christians should not be doing separately what we can do together. Wexford became a byword for active ecumenism, and Father Jim Fegan the administrator and myself initiated many community projects. In too many places Christian unity week is paraded out once a year and then forgotten. One of my initiatives was to start a four day Christmas fast outside the church on the four days before Christmas. This effort to help charities and cancer research received wonderful community support. Jim Fegan joined me for the last two years after nine years on my own. I had never asked any clergy to join me as I felt it would put pressure on them to say yes. When Jim offered to join me I was delighted, and we raised over twenty thousand euro each year.

It was said of John Wesley, founder of the Methodists, that people were 'strangely warmed' by his preaching. A nephew of mine once said that the worship was very real. I believe in incarnational preaching, and my preaching was subjective because I could only preach about what I had experienced. Too many of our churches are like poor restaurants which don't deserve to be patronised. The food is poor, stale and bland, the building is cold and has no toilet facilities. The seats are hard and uncomfortable. There is so little honesty in preaching, and the more honest we are, the more it encourages others to be honest. I shared in the pulpit the fears of cancer, the wrestling with depression and my own lack of love. An elderly lady was once livid after one of my sermons when I confessed my lack of love for others. Several weeks later her brother was dying in hospital. She had not spoken to him for years. I persuaded her to visit him, and I drove her to the hospital. She carried a lovely bunch of flowers. There were lots of tears, and a dying reconciliation. A former priest once said to me that he would like to see the aisles of our churches flowing with the tears of the penitents. Too many Te Deums and too few tears. Too much worship never touches the heart of man or woman.

There are three kinds of people who worship. There are those who love to praise God, then there are those who grin and bear it, or spend their time being critical of the priest. They bring negativity with them when they worship. The third group hear the message, cannot accept it, and fall away. Over the years in Wexford, St Iberius became the mother church for nine congregations, and began to draw inside its doors all kinds of different people. These people had no tribal allegiance, and brought uncomplicated freedom. Recently a bishop said that I opened the doors of the church and the people came in.

CHAPTER 24

Oscar Wilde and the Elgees

Charles Elgee was born in Durham in 1714, and was a bricklayer. He sailed to Ireland in the 1730s with his brother, where there was a building boom. They came to Dundalk, Co Louth. They quickly prospered. His youngest son, John Elgee was curate of St Iberius from 1790 to 1794 and rector from 1795 to 1823.

He held in plurality the archdeaconry of Leighlin. It was not uncommon on those days for clergy to hold several appointments. Generally they appointed a curate or an assistant to help. The St Iberius rectory stood in the town's bullring where there is a monument to the pikeman. The Diana Donnelly shop is the site of the former rectory.

Archdeacon John Elgee
Archdeacon Elgee nearly lost his life in the bitter Wexford rising of 1798 when, as John Melville writes, 'martial law was declared in Ireland to suppress the followers of the Society of United Irishmen'. In May 1798, the Wexford-Wicklow border became a bloodbath: men were flogged to make them reveal names of insurgents. The massacre and executions which followed caused the Wexford Rising. The rebels retreated to the town and the troops following them burned the hospital, its eighty sick and wounded inmates, and all the nearby houses.

In later years Jane Elgee, the Archdeacon's granddaughter told how 'he had avoided being killed at a time when few escaped butchering'. The rector was taking a service in his church when the rebels burst in, but one of them turned away their pikes and related a great kindness which the clergyman had rendered to his family. It was at once resolved that he and all his belongings should be untouched and a guard was placed at his home for his protection.

At St Brigid's Church, Rathaspeck, a few miles south of

Wexford, on the road to Johnstown Castle, you will find the memorial to Archdeacon John Elgee's 'beloved and lamented wife'. In this graveyard are six other tombstones to the many Elgees who died in Wexford.

The archdeacon's only daughter, Jane, married Captain Robert McClure of the 89th regiment. Their son Robert became an Arctic explorer, and discovered the North West Passage. He never returned to Wexford.

The archdeacon's eldest son, another Charles, opted for law rather than the church, and became a solicitor in Dublin. He married Sarah Kingsbury. Charles and Sarah Elgee returned to Wexford for their marriage in St Iberius Church on 23 December 1809. The service was conducted by Charles' younger brother, Richard, who is commemorated in the East window. The wedding celebrations combined with Christmas festivities must have given the couple a great send-off. Wexford was known for its parties, balls and musical evenings. One of the families in the parish, the Colcloughs, even had a small theatre on the top floor of their home for concerts and plays.

'Speranza' – Oscar Wilde's Mother

Charles and Sarah Elgee returned to Dublin. A deed of 1814 reveals that Charles Elgee was in debt. They had three children and their third child's death is recorded in St Iberius Church. The child was buried at Selskar. The birth date of the youngest child, Jane, is not recorded. She became known as the poet 'Speranza'. She married Doctor William Wilde, the brilliant eye and ear surgeon. Their younger son Oscar Wilde was the poet and dramatist. As a young woman, during the years of the great famine, Speranza electrified Ireland with her passionate tirades of verse and prose against the English.

Edith Elgee was the last member of an old Wexford family whose relatives had been rectors. The family once had money but Edith died in poor circumstances in a small bedsit. She told me how she used to cycle out to Curracloe House where her aunts lived and where they employed uniformed maids. Edith had a very prickly moustache and insisted on kissing the rector, who tried to avoid the greeting. After her death I found little cardboard boxes wrapped in elastic bands in her flat. Each box had half crown coins (about 20 cents), one for the church, one for Brownies and one for charities.

Edith's father had been a solicitor in Wexford, and her brother Richard was also a solicitor in Wexford. Dick died in middle age. Families come and families go. The Elgee name is perpetuated in the East window in St Iberius Church, Wexford.

CHAPTER 25

Bishop Brendan

A Bishop's Prayer
Tell my priests when I am gone,
O'er me to shed no tears
For I shall be no deader then
Than they have been for years.

Bishop Brendan loves that poem, and it fills his heart with laughter. Maybe there is an element of truth in it – 'for I shall be no deader then than they have been for years'! Certainly Brendan Comiskey was no dead priest and bishop, for he brought light and life wherever he appeared. In this year 2005 he was twenty-five years a bishop, but it was a very quiet anniversary.

There is a void in Wexford and the diocese of Ferns with the resignation of Brendan. At a function some years ago, at the height of the witch-hunt by Veronica Guerin towards Brendan, he came up to me with a serious face and asked me if Veronica Guerin was looking for him. In the midst of controversy he never lost his sense of humour. When Veronica Guerin was murdered on the Naas Road, the spotlight was taken off Brendan Comiskey, and life seemed to return to normality for him.

Veronica Guerin was a journalist with the *Irish Independent* newspapers. Fearless and courageous, she tried to expose the wealthy drug barons in Ireland. For this crusade she probably lost her life. She also drew attention to clerical abuse in Ferns diocese and the role of Bishop Brendan in the saga. However, the nightmare was to return with much greater media attention some time on.

Brendan hailed from farming stock in Co Monaghan, and has an intense love for his native county. It was there, surrounded by family loved ones that he found solace and rest when the long knives were out. Patrick Kavanagh also grew up in Co

Monaghan in Inniskeen, a son of the farm. He wrote prolifically about his native county, and made it known to a wider audience. Bishop Brendan was forever quoting Kavanagh's poetry. They shared a common heritage, they both suffered from the disease of alcoholism, they both were individualists, and misunderstood and sometimes rejected by those who crossed their paths. In a way they were both lonely, passionate men. Brendan brooding in the bishop's house in Summerhill, Wexford, and Patrick Kavanagh, cigarette in mouth, sitting on a lonely bench along the Grand Canal at Baggot Street Bridge, Dublin.

In a recently published book on Patrick Kavanagh's prose, the writer tackles a self-portrait. Kavanagh wrote, 'I have tried to find a technique through which a man might reveal himself without embarrassment. There are two successful examples of this technique – *Don Quixote* and Joyce's *Ulysses*. Sancho Panza and Mr Bloom are the private lives of two public men. We have all done mean and ugly things and nearly always these sins should be confessed because of the damage they have done. My life has been a failure till I woke this morning. I saw a wonder question-mark:

There is today
And tomorrow.'

He is remembering sins and failures of the past 'but there is today and tomorrow.' For Brendan as he begins a new life, divested of power and status, there is 'today and tomorrow'. Now seventy years of age, he would have reached retirement in any event. Those close to him say that he is lonely, and misses being an active bishop.

The BBC programme, *Suing the Pope*, some three years ago, on the priestly sex scandals in Ferns diocese was the catalyst that led to Brendan Comiskey's resignation. When he made his alcoholism known to his people and when he returned to the diocese of Ferns after treatment, it seemed that all would be well. He acquitted himself well at a national press conference in St Peter's College, Wexford, the scene of much sexual abuse. However, his previous disappearance from the diocese disturbed people. A diocesan information officer was asked by RTÉ if he was aware that Bishop Comiskey had a drinking problem, and replied 'not to my knowledge'.

Brendan left for treatment in the USA and when he returned from treatment he was a transformed person. He could talk 'eyeball to eyeball', and he could listen. He attended local Alcoholics Anonymous meetings, and was a great help to other members. He attended a Church of Ireland synod of Ferns at the Ferrycarrig Hotel, Wexford, and he electrified what would have been another deadly boring diocesan event. 'Ladies and gentlemen, I am an alcoholic. When you are on the ground, nobody can kick you any lower.' He reminded me of my diocesan bishop in Virginia, USA who confessed to us at a retreat 'I am an alcoholic.' The rest of the business at that Wexford synod that day seemed irrelevant. A burning social issue had invaded the privacy of a stuffy exclusive ecclesiastical occasion. It would never be the same again. Bishop Brendan had brought incarnation, and he had incarnated the gospel for us that day. A Roman Catholic bishop had enlightened a predictable Church of Ireland gathering.

Many of his senior clergy expressed strong views that Brendan should go. He had rocked the boat, and caused them embarrassment. They gave him little loyalty – the knives were out. He was never happy among the conservative phalanx in his diocese, and always seemed drawn to the younger priests with newer ideas and fresh thinking.

He had succeeded a conservative bishop, Donal Herlihy, who had the ideal combination for rural Ireland, conservatism and friendliness. Herlihy was also a theologian, trained in Rome. Travelling to South America to visit his missionary priests, Bishop Herlihy said to an Alitalia executive friend of mine on the plane, 'God it's great to get away from Ferns!' Herlihy was a fine interpreter of scripture and I can still remember a talk he gave at a quiet day in Carne, Co Wexford on Yahweh and *Kurios*. 'He is Lord.' Herlihy was the last RC bishop that I remember wearing lace gloves. He once came to an event at our rectory, and wrote a gracious letter of thanks to my wife Jean – one of few bishops to write thanks.

Acceptance
When I received an invitation from the bishop's secretary to come up to the bishop's house on Easter Monday 2002, my family

pleaded with me not to go. They did not want me to identify
with a bishop who might affect my ministry, and drag me into
the minefield of clerical child abuse. A grandfather of the
Jackman family who suffered through the abuse saga, John
Brown, was a lovely man. He was a parishioner of mine and
loved his golf and bowls. He reproached me for getting involved
in the Comiskey affair, and said it was none of my business. I
could not agree, and I think he admired my integrity. John at the
end of a long life was confused and upset by the publicity hoisted
on his family.

Bishop Brendan had always encouraged me and I was not
prepared to let him down now. When I ran a three day conference weekend on spirituality at the Talbot Hotel, Wexford,
Brendan chaired all the sessions, and never missed a minute. It
was a wonderful weekend of Christian fellowship, and our
speakers were John Pritchard, then Archdeacon of Canterbury,
now Bishop of Jarrow, and Father Jim Burke, an American
Dominican friend of mine, who spends his whole ministry travelling on retreats. The Roman Catholic priests strangely enough
were attracted to the freshness of Bishop Pritchard's imaginative
presentation, and were less enthused with the traditional but
spiritual approach of Father Jim Burke.

For ten years I had appeared on countless platforms with
Brendan, representing the Church of Ireland bishop or parish.
He once said of our relationship that 'I had the sacrament of
friendship.' It was a beautiful phrase. I was intent that Easter
Monday 2002, that I would not forsake him now, whatever the
consequences.

Arriving at the bishop's house it was like a long wake. His
friends and colleagues were there and many of them, including
myself, were in tears. Brendan kept saying as he tried to keep his
composure, 'I want a life, I want a life'. The pressure was mount-
ing on my friend, and I felt for his health and wellbeing. Was
Brendan any more to blame than the other bishops who never
dealt with clerical abuse? Had not the archbishop of Dublin
made financial payoffs to errant clergy? The archbishop had
been well informed of incidences of clerical abuse and did nothing about them. One of his priests, Michael Cleary, had fathered
children, and his family had denied it. Fortunately his mistress

told a psychiatrist, who made the truth known to the public. Another eminent psychiatrist castigated that psychistrist for betraying professional confidence, and had him hauled before his medical association. His truth and honesty were vindicated.

On the steps of the Bishop's House at Summerhill the press from city and country gathered on a rainy Monday morning to hear Brendan announce his resignation. I found it difficult to hold back my tears. We were losing a bishop who dared to be human, and who did not hide behind mitre and crozier. Anyway he wasn't very partial to mitres.

Bishop Comiskey's critics turned a blind eye to all the good things he had done. He stated that celibacy should be examined in the light of the disastrous fall in ordinations to the priesthood. For this statement he was called to Rome. He initiated with the Church of Ireland bishop, joint services and guidelines for inter-church baptisms and weddings. At the 1978 service of commemoration in Rowe Street Church, Wexford, with senators present from all over the world, he apologised for the Fethard-on-Sea boycott. Brendan, the prophet knew that the file on Fethard-on-Sea needed to be closed. His apology did that. Brendan made this apology before President Mary McAleese, who said that it was the most inspiring act of worship that she had ever attended. It was a truly uplifting act of worship.

At the opening of the third level facility at St Peter's College, in conjunction with Carlow Regional Technical College, at the press conference Bishop Comiskey said: 'There would be no future for Wexford without third level education.' In January 2002, at the Borough Council Mass in Rowe Street Church, he said: 'There is no such thing as a perfect politician, no more than there is a perfect bishop. There is a society that increasingly demands perfect priests to minister to them. It's alright to be imperfect.'

In Brendan's resignation speech he said that 'I can only assure you that I did my best. Clearly this was not good enough. I wish to apologise to each of those four men whose stories of abuse have been depicted in the recently broadcast documentary, *Suing the Pope*, and to all those who have been abused by priests of the diocese. I found Father Fortune (he later committed suicide at his home in New Ross) virtually impossible to deal with. Wherever Fr Fortune served he brought division and pain.'

'Having resigned my office as bishop I intend to undertake initially a period of personal discernment as I prepare for the next stage of my life. I call for the prayers of the people as I begin this journey.' An editorial in the local paper commented that it is 'sad that a man of such intelligence and promise has seen his career end in such a manner, and that for the moment at least, his many good deeds will be overshadowed by his failings in relation to the handling of the clerical sex abuse allegations.' Why didn't Brendan kick out Fortune earlier? Brendan spoke of 'the nightmare of what happened to those teenage boys, who were abused.'

Guilty or not Guilty?
Priests who were accused of sexual abuse were suspended subject to investigation. In some cases the Director of Public Prosecutions said that there was no case to answer. Another priest who openly confessed to sexual relations with a girl was permanently suspended. Some of the priests were sent abroad for sexual counselling. Though no case was ever proven or taken against some of them, they were never reinstated but 'retired'. One priest friend, who wrote a courageous letter to the local press, asked why one particular priest had not been reinstated. He was summoned before his ecclesiastical superior, and censured for going public. A fear has gripped the institutional church in Ferns diocese.

My heart goes out to these forgotten priests. Their names have been taken off the diocesan list, and they are not allowed to say Mass or wear clerical dress. One suspended priest friend wondered whether he could still play golf with the Ferns Clergy Golfing Society. I personally brought him to golf and encouraged him. These priests have been subjects of judge and jury. It this the behaviour of a loving church? Is there no compassion, no second chance? Jesus said, 'Neither do I condemn you, go and sin no more.'

Fr Jim Grennan, who was accused of sexual misconduct in Monageer, was once my neighbour, and we socialised together on many occasions. After dinner at my rectory one evening, as he was leaving he suddenly lifted his arms high and said, 'Oh, I'd love to be married.' He had enjoyed the warm hospitality, good companionship and delicious food of my wife Jean. Now he was on his way home to Poulpeasty nearby to an empty house. I loved that man. I find it hard to believe that he interfered with confirmation girls, though the facts are there. When he returned to the parish of Monageer, near Enniscorthy, for Confirmation, some of the parents of the girls concerned walked out. It was poor judgement on the bishop's part to have this controversial priest present on the altar that day.

Fr Jim Grennan died as did his brother, a priest. Did they die of broken hearts? The Monageer saga was investigated by the South Eastern Health Board and the file ended up in Enniscorthy Garda Station. When Garda Headquarters in Dublin asked for the file, they were told that the file was mislaid. The Chief Commissioner of the Garda, asked to comment on the file said that if the Garda in Co Wexford had a case to answer then it would be rigorously investigated. What happened to the file on Monageer? There were probably those who did not want to see the church debased or denigrated in such fashion. We may never know.

My first real contact with Father Sean Fortune was on a Sunday afternoon when he invited me to give the homily at one of his 'healing services'. He wore an appallingly ugly cope, and was liturgically overdressed. My wife came with me. Afterwards, at the presbytery, ladies in the parish had prepared a sumptuous meal and the wine flowed. My wife Jean said that she felt he was an evil man, and she did not want to be in his company again. She is a very intuitive and perceptive person, and her doubts were proven as time unfolded. As Bishop Brendan said, Fortune brought trouble.

The BBC programme, *Suing the Pope*, which focused on four young men who had been abused by Ferns clergy, blew the top off the festering sore of rumour, innuendo and accusation. Fr Sean Fortune, one of the abusing priests, was the worst bad apple in the barrel. Fortune had been a priest in Ferns diocese during the episcopate of Bishop Herlihy, who found Fortune impossible to deal with. Bishop Comiskey was bitterly criticised by parents and parishioners in his diocese. Letters of complaint were sent to the bishop who allegedly never answered them or acted on them. He did try to send Fortune for therapy.

In the BBC documentary one of the most damning moments was when the woman reporter tried to ask Brendan questions on the steps of Rowe Street Church in Wexford. Brendan may not have realised in the euphoria of the moment that he had turned his back on the reporter and walked away. The behaviour won him no friends, but he may have been close to breaking point. The end seemed near – the *Suing the Pope* programme was the catalyst that brought about the bishop's resignation. It was only a question of time before everything collapsed. I had written to Bishop Brendan the previous week, pleading with him to stand his ground and dismiss resignation from his mind. It was all to no avail – he had made his decision, he had had enough.

Amid rumours of my retirement, Brendan wrote a touching letter with words from Rabbi Ben Ezra (1864):

'Grow old along with me
The best is yet to be
The last of life for which the first was made,
Our times are in His hands
Who saith 'a whole I planned
Youth shows but half, trust God
See all nor be afraid.'

Very few of Brendan Comiskey's episcopal colleagues offered him any public support. They may have done so in private. It is amazing that a hierarchy of which he was a member for eighteen years had abandoned him. Had word come from Rome to let him drown? Hadn't he caused them enough publicity in Rome over celibacy?

I wrote at the time in *The Irish Times* that a light had gone out in the diocese of Ferns, and Wexford doesn't seem the same without him. In that paper I wrote: 'Too many prelates preach a gospel of predictability. Safe men are selected who will not rock the boat. Is it any wonder the world is turning its back on institutional religion? The ship is rudderless and becalmed. There seems to be no room for the human bishop of Ferns.'

Bishop Brendan was a media man, and the media crucified him. Now we are left without a bishop, and it is safe to bet that a card carrying person will be appointed who will not rock the boat or raise delicate issues. For Brendan I hope that 'the best is yet to be'.

'A Great Sense of Wellbeing'

I suppose that the best barometer of a bishop's popularity or otherwise is to interview his clergy. One diocesan priest, a self-confessed alcoholic, and a lovely man, told me when asked for a comment, that whenever he left Bishop Brendan's presence he felt a great sense of wellbeing. He always felt better for having been in his presence. I first came to know this warm-hearted priest through golf, and a shared interest in gardening. I was delighted to be able to give him the 'Rambling Rector' rose for his presbytery garden.

Two other senior priests that I interviewed spoke warmly of Bishop Brendan. I thought that they would be very critical, as the senior clergy were never close to their bishop. One had been chairman of the council of priests when Brendan came as bishop to Ferns. He felt that the bishop should never have resigned, and that the issue was badly handled. Bishop Comiskey had had no experience as a secular priest and no financial experience. He had been part of a religious order, which provided funds when needed. As a member of a religious community he did not have to handle money. The bishop may well have laid out many funds to reorganise the diocese. One of his most prophetic actions was to found Christian Media Trust under the umbrella of South East Radio and the advent of local radio franchises. He got a foot in the door at the very beginning, bought shares in South East Radio, and set up a recording studio. He also involved other denominations in the project, and never asked for any financial contribution. As a rector I greatly appreciated this radio ministry, which on a *per capita* basis had a larger listening audience on a Sunday morning that RTÉ Radio. Here, again when the question of money reared its head in relation to Bishop Comiskey's spending, the question was continually asked where the bishop got the money to invest in local radio. Some felt that the sale of land for building, adjacent to the bishop's house at Summerhill, Wexford, provided the necessary funds.

As to Fr Sean Fortune, who seemed to wield a Svengali-like influence over Bishops Herlihy and Comiskey, both senior priests admitted that Fortune should never have been ordained, but there was then a shortage of priests, and seminaries would take anybody. Now there are much stricter guidelines. The

Church of Ireland equally ordained priests that should never have been ordained, and here again it was a question of chronic shortage of clergy.

Fr Fortune only served under Bishop Herlihy for four years, up to the bishop's death in 1983. Fortune continually denied any impropriety which didn't help matters. There was a rumour that Fortune was close to Comiskey which was a fable. It was also insinuated that Fortune had a hold on the bishop and could bring him down.

Both senior priests felt that Bishop Herlihy had a greater affinity with the people, and that Bishop Brendan was not a good communicator and did not follow through his ideas. He had a poor methodology. He was narcissistic in that he always needed 'centre stage' and attention. He liked and encouraged self-adulation.

One of the unfortunate events in Bishop Comiskey's episcopate was the death of the diocesan accountant who took his own life. His son had been abused by one of the diocesan priests. A papal knight who was a friend of Bishop Comiskey had to live with the dreadful abuse of one of his sons by Fr Sean Fortune.

CHAPTER 26

'Mid pleasures and palaces

'Mid pleasures and palaces
Though we may roam
Be it ever so humble,
There's no place like home.

One of the most emotive, controversial and divisive experiences in church life was the disposal of the Palace in Kilkenny, the residence of bishops for centuries. The news of the possible disposal of the house was leaked at a function in Galway, when a member of the Heritage Council stated that the council was in discussion with the Church Body with a view to taking over the palace as a headquarters for the Heritage Council. Word travels fast in Ireland through a kind of 'bush telegraph' and news of these discussions reached Co Wexford rapidly. I was concerned, like many others, as several years previously the dioceses had unanimously decided to retain the palace.

Bishop John Neill was at the beginning of his ministry in the diocese when the palace issue erupted. When I asked him for his views on the disposal of the house, he said that there were points for and against parting with the building. It was all very difficult for him as his wife had contracted cancer, and it must have been difficult for her to cope with the large building. Thankfully she has recovered. Those of us who objected to the transfer of the palace were looked on as rebels by the ecclesiastical authorities. As time passed it did seem to many of us that Bishop Neill favoured the disposal of the house and agreed with the decision of the Church Body to sell the house. A mole in Church House told me that concerted efforts were made in the legal department to expedite the transfer of the palace to the Heritage Council. The dye was cast.

In the fourteenth century Bishop Ledred had demolished three churches outside the city walls of Kilkenny, and he used the stone to build an Episcopal Palace beside St Canice's

Cathedral. The floor plan shows the thick walls of the old square tower and the adjoining house. By 1661 this area had become derelict and Bishop Charles Este, appointed bishop in 1735, renovated the building. The façade of 1735 looked very much like it is today, except that the roof has been raised. The magnificent entrance hall and its vaulting are particularly beautiful. Twenty five years later Bishop Pococke built the graceful robing room in the garden. The beautiful dining room and drawing room upstairs were probably added in 1779 when the then bishop's wife said that the house was small and gloomy. When Bishop McAdoo was appointed to the diocese in the early 1960s he had one wing of the house demolished. He also designed an exquisite chapel on the ground floor, with the same vaulted ceilings. It is indeed an exquisite building in the centre of Kilkenny with the lovely DeMontmorency pleasure gardens which that family had made available for the bishop. The palace also has ample parking for cars, while the cathedral has no space for parking, especially for special services.

At a diocesan synod in Ferns on 25 September 1873 it was agreed that it is desirable that the palace at Kilkenny with curtilage and garden should be purchased for the use of the bishop. It was also agreed that 'the purchase money for the purchase of the palace should be borrowed from the Representative Body, and shall be charged in equal proportion to each diocese.' (Before the Church of Ireland was disestablished [became independent] in 1870, most Church of Ireland properties belonged to the Crown, and had to be bought from the British government.) It was also agreed that in the event of the palace being purchased from joint resources, the diocese separating shall be restored a reasonable proportion of the cost. One can see that in 1873 the independent diocese of Ferns was very much involved in the united dioceses of Ossory, Ferns and Leighlin.

The cathedral, palace, deanery and library make up the last example of a complete cathedral close in Ireland. The financial burden of retaining the palace was given as a reason for disposal. This argument is nonsense as there was a very good income from the sale of the bishop's house in Waterford in the 1970s. Cashel also had funds from the sale of its Episcopal Palace, and all these funds could be used to maintain Kilkenny. The parishes in the six dioceses never had any trouble providing funds for the maintenance of the palace. The people saw the house as a focus of the diocese, and enjoyed using the house and grounds on diocesan occasions, when invited by successive bishops and their wives.

Some bishops enjoyed the house more than others, and made it a real home for their families. Bishop McAdoo said he wanted to lie between the two buildings that he loved best – the cathedral and the palace. His wish was granted. Bishop John Armstrong, his successor, did not want to move into the house at all, and eventually was loathe to leave Waterford. It would have taken a crane to move him. If Kilkenny was not to be used as a home for the bishop, then Waterford would have made an ideal centre and focus.

Bishop Noel Willoughby insisted on living in the palace and demanded the keys of the house. He was prepared to reject the bishopric if he was not allowed to live with his family there. The Willoughbys made it a real home, entertaining lavishly, and enjoyed seventeen happy years there.

We set up a petition for people to sign who objected to the transfer of the palace to the Heritage Council. We in Ferns diocese, with the blessing of a palace committee which included Lord Dermot Donegal, sent in over one thousand signatures to both our archbishops and political representatives. None of them acknowledged our petition.

The plan involved handing over the palace to the Heritage Council, and in return the government would build a modern house in the grounds. When Bishop Armstrong criticised the retention of the palace, Bishop McAdoo said that Armstrong had 'a villa mentality'. A meeting of both councils was held at Butler House, Kilkenny, to vote on the future of the palace. We were given separate coloured voting cards. Ferns voted to retain the house while Cashel and Ossory voted to dispose of the house. The Ferns vote, we believed, cancelled any change. We were quickly disillusioned. What subsequently happened was the shabbiest legislation ever. The legal affairs committee of the Church of Ireland ruled that the palace was only the concern of the diocese in which the house stood. The diocese of Ossory only numbers about four clergy, while we in Ferns number ten. For

over one hundred and seventy five years Ferns had been inti-
mately involved in the affairs of the palace in Kilkenny and now
we were purposely excluded. Who initiated this ruling by the
legal affairs committee? Not one of the bench of bishops showed
any support for our cause. Archbishop Eames rubber stamped
the issue, and did not allow us to raise the matter at General
Synod, as it was sub-judice. There was a deafening silence from
the people of Kilkenny. One titled lady in Kilkenny did sign our
petition, while others were afraid to take a line opposed to the
establishment and were nervous of signing.

The whole saga drew a wedge between Ferns and Ossory,
and Ferns people are disenchanted with what has happened. It
will take time to heal. It has driven Ferns diocese deeper into in-
dependence. We believed that luxury accommodation could
have been provided for a bishop's family upstairs in the palace,
while the ground floor could be used for administration. It is a
ludicrous situation. We have given away valuable parking. I
wonder what is the commercial value of the palace property
today. Five million? Ten million? And we gave away six centuries of our heritage.

A long-standing friend, Peter Barrett, Dean of Waterford was
appointed as our bishop, and he has been pouring oil on troubled waters and re-establishing contacts and confidence. Peter,
during my latest fight with cancer, has constantly phoned and
written to find out about my welfare. He has no axe to grind re-
garding the Palace, and I'm sure he would live in a mobile home
if required. He is thoughtful, kind and generous. He has vision,
knows what needs to be done, but is wise enough to know that
'the mills of God grind slowly'. I hope he does 'what's important
and not what's urgent', and that he does not burn himself out.
Peter is the tenth bishop I have served under.

The Palace has now been handed over to the Heritage
Council, which is building a new Bishop's residence in the
Palace grounds. We lost the struggle to retain the historic resi-
dence. Democracy was given a poor innings.

CHAPTER 27

The Red Mercedes

(A true story. The people's names have been changed to protect anonymity.)

Cara looked out the window and gazed at the russet leaves falling off the big chestnut trees which surrounded the palatial farmhouse. Dad was no longer able to farm and Nicky, her favourite brother, carried on the work. Cara and Nicky used to have great chats together, but now he was married and life had changed. Poor Mum spent all her time looking after Dad – dancing to his every call. Cara hated the way that her mother had been walked on all the years but at least her mother found consolation in her religion and her Bible. Nicky never asked for much and lived in the shadow of his sick father. Life here on the farm and in the nearby town of Kingsport never changed – Cara was sick and tired of rural Ireland, the potholed roads, the broken down walls, the broken windows, the pious priests and parsons.

Cara looked in the mirror at herself. She was now twenty-five years old and single. She knew she was attractive by the way men looked at her, but she was tired of going to dances and being pawed by some drunken farmer at the end of the night. It took the drink to give the men courage, but there was no way that Cara was going to be raped in the back seat of a battered Toyota. She turned away from the mirror and began to pack the last bits and pieces into her stylish new travelling bag, a parting gift from the nurses in the hospital in Belfast. Her hospital badge lay on her bed and the shining silver sparkled in the light overhead – she suddenly began to think of the four years of study and the mutilated bodies that she cared for so near to the Falls Road.

Cara closed the bag and took one final look at her room and all the little mementoes of her childhood – the teddy bear, her doll's cot, and leather school bag. It was the most expensive school bag in the shop and Daddy had insisted that she have the very best. It was still almost perfect. She went downstairs – Dad was not up yet – he never got up now before lunch. Cara slipped into her Dad's bedroom and bending down she gave him a farewell kiss. He gave her a warm hug and began sobbing – she felt it was time to go. Mum was reading her Bible in the kitchen – they didn't say much – a brief hug and Cara hurried for the yard door. Down the long avenue she walked – it had never had a load of gravel laid on it in all her lifetime. Her father and brother never spent money foolishly. Reaching the main road she waited for the once weekly bus that went to Dublin – a bone shaking journey if ever there was one. She was the only passenger on the bus. It finally reached Busaras where she hailed a taxi for Dublin Airport. It all seemed such a lifeless goodbye to Ireland – no farewell party, no parting gifts, no telephone calls, and not even a call from her rector. Cara felt she was like flotsam caught in a backwater and now it was time to float on out into the wide world. She'd waited long enough for a job in Kingsport and there was no way that she would lower herself to collect the dole. It was all for the best – there wasn't an eligible Church of Ireland man in the parish and marrying a Roman Catholic man was out of the question so near the border. Her parents had tried to marry her off to a Protestant farmer in his sixties but she had escaped that noose.

Sitting in the jumbo jet, she looked down at the tiny green fields below – they made all her problems seem meaningless. The long journey to Sydney, Australia, gave her time to think – the movie, *Love Story*, took her thoughts far away from Ireland. Cara was excited about the new job as theatre sister at the general hospital in Sydney. When she had cleared customs the administrator of the hospital, Peter Pollock, met her and took her bags. 'Care for a drink Cara?' asked Peter. 'Delighted', said Cara. One drink led to another and Cara felt a new warmth for this gentle Australian. She felt that he was much older than herself – maybe even forty. Thus began a romance that lasted almost all of the ten wonderful years that Cara spent in Sydney. Even when she left the hospital and took up a job as a saleswoman, the romance continued. She knew that Peter had a serious drinking problem but that was not uncommon in Australia. Cara was not to know that Peter would die a week after she returned to Ireland in 1985 – her first visit home in ten years. Among his possessions was found an engagement ring that he had planned to give Cara. However, he knew that he was dying and he never proposed to her.

Cara was now almost thirty five. The fact dawned on her as she filled in motor insurance forms. Outside the taxation office her red mini stood proudly. She had had to save a lot of Aussie dollars to buy it but her travelling expenses from her new employer in Belfast would soon help to maintain it. She was tired of nursing and liked the challenge of her new work selling life insurance. She had made lots of money selling insurance in Australia and she could do it here in Belfast. Cara had found a cosy flat in Knock, near the sloping hills of South Belfast. It was a nice quiet place away from the violence, even if she shuddered as she passed the RUC detention centre at Castlereagh down the road. Her flat overlooked the main road to Roselawn cemetery and the daily funerals caused by the troubles – would it ever end? But then she was used to violence and many was the battered body that she tended in Sydney General Hospital. There it was Aboriginal and white – here it was prod and popehead … Funny that the same blood ran in each.

Life was good in Belfast and Cara had saved a lot of money in two years – especially from the generous commission. In 1987 it dawned on her that she was now nearing forty and the dreaded middle years. She was still a striking looking woman and plenty of men still asked her out. She travelled down regularly to see her parents in Kingsport but there was more life in the cemetery than in the main street. All the young men and women were gone – it was as if a whole generation had been wiped out. Lemass's dream had become a nightmare. The only fixtures in the rural town were the despairing faces of the unemployed who propped up the street corners and stared vacantly into space. Cara thought of the frigid looking churches which only came to life when there were funerals. She thought of the comfortable priests and parsons who moved about in a quiet vacuum and seemed to change nothing. Cara didn't hold out much hope for the Republic and God help the single girls who wanted male

company – nothing had changed since she left in 1975. If anything matters were worse.

Cara waved goodbye to her Mum and Dad and set out on the
twisty road to the border – it was always a major job navigating
the potholes to the border and then the smooth bliss of Northern
Ireland roads. The para on duty at the army post gave her a
warm smile and chatted her up for a date. But Cara wasn't interested and it created more problems than its worth to get mixed
up with a British soldier. The constant fear of murder would
drive her crazy. She was more interested in other things as she
quickly reached the motorway near Armagh. A girlfriend in the
office had invited her to a disco in Crawfordsburn Rugby Club
tonight and she was looking forward to a social evening. She
hadn't really had a steady since Australia and she still could not
forget Peter – dear Peter, darling Peter. A tear ran down her
cheek – the memory was still painful.

The rugby club was packed with burly pint drinkers when
Cara arrived. She was wearing a lovely leather dress that Peter
had bought her for her birthday. Her friend Hilary was busily
engaged with her amorous boyfriend – it looked as if Cara was
going to be a lonely wallflower for the evening. She sat at a stool
at the bar and ordered a gin and tonic. Suddenly a big curly
haired rugby player came up and sat down beside her. 'I'm
Stephen Rudd,' he said. 'I'm single, I'm lonely, I think you're
beautiful and I'd like you to dance.' Cara had never met anyone
like this before but there was a gentleness about him that ap-
pealed to her. They spent the evening dancing together and Cara
allowed him to see her home. She was so swept off her feet that
she invited him in for coffee. Stephen told her that he worked for
the civil service in Stormont. As they parted at the front door
they exchanged a goodnight kiss.

The Tears of Things
That night was the first of many nights and it was on New Year's
Eve 1987 at the stroke of midnight that Stephen asked Cara to
marry him. They drove out to the sea at Bangor and it was there
that Stephen confessed to Cara that he was a detective in the
RUC. 'Civil Service' was a convenient cover for members of the
RUC. Cara felt a funny feeling in her tummy but she knew that

whatever the cost she was not going to lose this chance of happiness. Stephen was the kindest and gentlest man that she had ever met. She had always wanted to be married at home in the South, but marrying a member of the RUC would make it more difficult, let alone the security risks. Stephen would always be in danger in the South of Ireland, and the border area where she lived was full of provos. She decided to tell nobody of her wedding plans and the actual date of her wedding – Saturday 3rd September, her birthday. She felt the pain of not even telling her parents but it seemed best for the safety of Stephen's life.

I answered the rectory doorbell as I surfaced after a Sunday afternoon nap. I didn't like visitors on Sunday afternoons but the sight of Cara and Stephen on the doorstep delighted me. I wasn't a bit surprised to hear that they wanted to arrange a wedding date. Cara felt for security reasons that she should be married at her home and that would require a special licence from the bishop. Her home would be well away from the publicity of the parish church. It so happened my friend, Bishop Bernard from Swaziland, southern Africa was staying with me after attending the Lambeth Conference of bishops in Canterbury, Kent. We had first met on a train to Canterbury when a warm friendship developed between us. Bernard is now retired, and living near the Swaziland border with Mozambique. Before Stephen and Cara left, the bishop quietly and graciously gave the couple his blessing. As they left the rectory I gazed enviously at Stephen's beautiful red Mercedes – I would never own a car like that.

It was only two weeks later that I answered another call – this time on the phone. It was Cara in tears – Stephen had just been blown up in Lurgan in his lovely red Mercedes. He had just paid a call on his mother to see how she was. 'This is not the time for words,' she said to me. I felt only numbness and hopelessness. This same feeling filled my soul as I crossed the border and headed for Stephen's funeral in Belfast. The church grounds were surrounded with armed RUC and troops. With my southern registration plate I was stopped at least four times and questioned suspiciously – the northern mourners didn't get that treatment. Yet again, another bishop mouthed platitudes and on this occasion belted out the unionist cause. The bishop attacked the provos viciously – when would the ecclesiastics ever learn that violence only reaps violence? I almost dared to challenge the bishop in the church grounds but I didn't get the chance. That night that bishop's sermon received banner headlines in the *Belfast Telegraph*. Quiet, shy Stephen needed no bishop at his parting but on the other side of death he could not triumph over ecclesiastical politics.

Stephen had been decorated for bravery many times – Cara never knew. The black procession headed for Roselawn cemetery. I remembered taking funerals there when it first opened – virgin land, now quickly filling up. The troubles had hastened that natural occurrence. Cara stepped forward to the edge of the grave and threw her parting gift in the gaping brown hole – an orchid that she had treasured from their last dinner dance. Stephen had given it to her when he called to pick her up that night. Later at Stephen's home his mother gave Cara the engagement ring that had been in his wallet. Stephen had intended to give it to her on the evening he was murdered. She did not know but Stephen had reserved a table for dinner at a hotel the very evening of his death.

I drove quietly out of Belfast and back south to the sleepy town of Kingsport. My thoughts were with Cara – twice engaged – twice a kind of widow. Why is fate so cruel? Why are so many marriages hell on earth and others do not get the chance to turn hell into heaven? I stopped for a coffee near the bloody, bloody border. I took out my black diary and crossed out the date of Cara's wedding. She still had the white copy of the wedding service that I had sent her – 'to love and to cherish, till death us do part'. I took out of my wallet a kindly cheque that my generous bishop had sent me to spend on myself – my own bishop would have had different words to share at the funeral, but then he wasn't born under an Ulster mushroom! I went up to the counter and bought a bottle of Tia Maria for my wife, her particular poison. Outside I clambered into my twenty-year-old Renault, let out the clutch and began to put many miles between myself and death.

CHAPTER 28

The Finale

February 2004 arrived rapidly. I found it difficult to realise that exactly eleven years ago I had received a phone call to ask me if I was interested in coming to Wexford as rector. The years had flown by and I had enjoyed the most fulfilling years of my ministry. I never dreamt that I would find such fulfilment in the latter days of my ministry. This was the first time that I felt remorse leaving a rectory, because we had put much energy and finance into restoring, extending and beautifying the house and garden. One rector may maintain a rectory while another may let it go to rack and ruin. In the west of Ireland there was a very autocratic bishop who visited a certain rectory. The rector was not interested in gardening. The bishop wrote to the rector afterwards and told him that he was not to grow silage on the front lawn! The bishop also requested that when he visited the parish again, there should be a churchwarden on hand to carry the bishop's case into the vestry.

Now I retire in Wexford to live in a fine old house, close to the town. Upstairs on a windowpane are scratched the names of four Hadden boys of the 19th century. George, Dick, Willie and Addison. The year was 1893. It puts into perspective our span of time and how families come and go. The Haddens were a Methodist family who had drapery shops in Dungarvan, Wexford and Carlow. The shops have long disappeared. In the drawing room, Hadden 1882 is also scratched on a windowpane.

I presume that this is the house where I will end my days. This house in Richmond Terrace was also at one time a maternity home, run by Molly Lowney. We brought a friend into the living room, and she pointed to the corner where her son Paul was born. Paul is now a priest. The house has great sense of life about it – new life. This may well be due to the fact that many beautiful young lives began here. My son Norman has helped us financially to live here. He once wrote of his gratitude for his education and he has repaid it many times over. On our first trip to New Zealand he gave us generous spending money from his first salary cheque. We were at a wedding and Norman Junior wrote on an enclosed card, 'As you have always been generous to me I want to repay your generosity.' It was a touching thought. We have been blessed with four generous children.

My last official weekend as Rector of Wexford was a hectic affair. Some days earlier I had received a letter from the Wexford Chamber of Industry and Commerce telling me that I had been awarded a Vodafone Passion for the World Around Us Award. The citation read:

'Firstly, congratulations on being the recipient of the Vodafone Passion for the World Around Us Award.

The aim of the award is to acknowledge people who demonstrate a keen commitment to improving the world in which we live. It is to honour people who have made a positive difference to their community.

You have been nominated for this award in recognition of your outstanding service to Wexford. You have played a key role in fostering links between the local churches of different denominations and raising awareness of the similarities between the faiths.

As a result of your vision, St Iberius Church has become well established as a popular venue for arts and cultural events year round and it plays a key role during Wexford Festival Opera. This coupled with opening the Church for a variety of guest speakers to talk about their faith and spirituality.

The annual fast that you undertake for charity has raised substantial amounts for charities in Wexford and abroad.

Your involvement in Music for Wexford is creating an appreciation of classical music throughout the year, bringing musicians of the highest quality to Wexford.

You have worked quietly and tirelessly to change attitudes towards religion, the arts and to raise awareness of the needs of others. It was the unanimous decision of the judging panel that you should receive this aware in recognition of your tremendous contribution to life in Wexford.'

The Vodafone Manager made the presentation of a beautiful solid silver sculpture of dancing ballet dancers, by an Irish artist, in St Iberius Church on that Friday morning. I was very humbled by this community award and recognition.

On the Friday evening the parish hosted a dinner in our honour at the new Riverbank Hotel in Wexford, and I received a beautiful painting by Elizabeth Brophy. Elizabeth Brophy, an Australian, is now in her eighties and living in Co Wicklow. My friend 'art enthusiast', Eddie O'Reilly, introduced us to Elizabeth's work at an exhibition in Galway. Elizabeth has now become our most outstanding impressionist as her work has been published in a lovely new book. I fell in love with the impressionists in the Quai d'Orsay museum in Paris when I visited the city on our 40th wedding anniversary, a present from our family. I also received a generous cheque from the parish. Rosslare parish also made me a lovely presentation.

On the Saturday evening the Mayor, Dominic Kiernan and Borough Council hosted a civic reception in my honour at the Municipal buildings. Here again I received a beautiful sculpture of a maiden with running water by Genesis of Mullingar. Speaking at the event the Mayor said, 'We are gathered here to pay tribute to a great and good, true man of God, a priestly priest who has brought a new dimension to his church here in Wexford. After Norman's appointment to Wexford he was diagnosed with cancer. This did not deter this special person, and because of this very positive attitude and with the skills of a gifted consultant, Norman recovered. On behalf of the people of Wexford, I thank you sincerely for the unprecedented role you have played since you came amongst us and I wish you both a very peaceful retirement still living amongst us here in Wexford.' I deeply appreciate the honour paid to me by the Borough Council as they are a group of people whom I have grown to love over the years and whose company I have greatly enjoyed.

On Sunday morning in St Iberius Church the Borough Council again turned out at a Eucharist to give thanks for my ministry in Wexford. It was an occasion that I will never forget for few clergy are honoured in this way.

The Chairman of the Board of Management of the school, Peter Hudson made me a generous presentation of a sculpture of children and a wallet of notes.

CHAPTER 29

'I love you, all will be well'

Three deeply religious experiences happened to me in my long life, which have confirmed for me the presence of a loving God. The first experience happened when I was in an intensive care ward in the City Hospital, Belfast. I thought that I was dying. I felt myself being carried over a great divide. It was very beautiful there and I did not want to come back. Next morning a Welsh doctor told me that they thought they had lost me during the night. A man had died in the bed opposite me that night. I have never feared death since that experience and the experience has helped others to die.

The second event was after a service on Pentecost Sunday in Killane, Co Wexford. We had a very uplifting family communion. As I drove along the side of the Blackstairs Mountains, I heard angels singing. I saw no sight of human life. I stopped the car and listened to the heavenly music. It lasted for at least five minutes.

The third special experience happened recently when I began my cancer treatment. I was looking out my bedroom window (the very panes of glass with the Haddens boys' names) early in the morning towards the harbour when God spoke to me: 'I love you, all will be well.' These words brought me great comfort, as we had to deal very suddenly with my son-in-law Jonathan's brain tumour. I never prayed with such intensity as the night in December, on Jonathan's daughter Maya's birthday, when he collapsed. Jonathan is recovering, marvellously well. 'I love you, all will be well.'

I was finding retirement difficult. I had no energy and had lost two stone weight. I had also lost interest in eating. I assumed that retirement was causing me my difficulties but it was not so. I would not go to the doctor. We get our cars serviced regularly, but rarely have our bodies serviced until they need

medical attention. Thankfully a friend, Dr Miriam Geraghty, noticed my white face and wrote letters to my doctor, local consultant in Wexford Hospital and my oncologist in Dublin,
Desmond Carney. Dr Carney saw me immediately and was concerned about my weight loss. He took me in that day for a full
week's battery of tests. The diagnosis was that I had malignant
lymphomas in the bone marrow. I was devastated – the cancer
had returned after eleven years and it was little wonder that I
was not enjoying retirement.

A Wonder Drug

A course of treatment was programmed with eight three-week
treatment modules. One of the drugs is rituximat, which belongs
to a group of cancer drugs known as monoclonal antibodies and
is well explained in a handout leaflet in the oncology department. It is used to treat several types of non-Hodgkin's lymphomas. Rituximat is sometimes given by itself to people whose
cancer has come back after chemotherapy. It is given in combination with chemotherapy. Monoclonal antibodies are used to
try and destroy some types of cancer cells while causing little
harm to normal cells. They recognise certain proteins that are
found on the surface of particular cancer cells. The monoclonal
antibody recognises the protein and 'locks' on to it. (Like a key
in a lock.) This may then trigger the body's immune system to
attack the cancer cells and sometimes cause the cells to destroy
themselves. After the first treatment the drugs are given in the
outpatients clinic which is wonderful as it avoids long stays in
hospital beds. Side effects of the drugs, I have discovered
through use, are numbness in fingers, coughing and breathless-
ness. I feel better now than I have felt for years, my appetite has
returned, my weight has stabilised, and my bloods are normal.
Now I am about to face hopefully my final treatment and bone
marrow test. This course of treatment compared with eleven
years ago seems much milder and less intense.

How are you enjoying retirement? I suppose it is a very natural question, but I confess that it is only now after cancer that I
am beginning to enjoy life in a new way. I am so glad that I have
used time over the last eleven years to collect funds for Mater
Cancer research fund. I do miss contact with the school children,

but I am blessed to have six grandchildren in the local primary school. I enjoy playing chess with my grandsons, and playing with model railways. We have all become members of the Wexford Model Railway Society in an old disused church near Wexford.

I miss baptisms and weddings, and sharing in the major events of family lives. I miss the freedom of knocking on doors and visiting parish families.

Cancer wards are generally out of sight on the top floor of hospitals. I have one strange custom. Each time I pass the hospital morgue in Wexford I say to it, 'You're not going to get me, you're not going to get me!'

Today is the first day of the rest of my life. I have closed the door on one chapter of my life and set out on another far less known way. I now have the freedom to do things that I never had the time to do. I have left my work in Wexford behind. One sows, another reaps.

As I set off for Australia and New Zealand I am leaving behind my greatest contribution to my life's work. I am setting out to travel which is one of my greatest delights. I love airports, train stations and ferry ports. I love watching aeroplanes, trains and ships arriving and departing. Maybe this is the escapist within me. I love standing over Rosslare Harbour in Co Wexford and watching ships on the horizon, heading for port, coming home. However I hate those moments with family at air terminals when its time to say goodbye, my stomach knots, and tears are at hand.

I am now 70 yeas of age, and I have lived twenty-nine years longer than my father William. I have always regretted never knowing him. I am grateful that I have lived long enough to see my own four children become adults and parents themselves. I'm not a lover of death or funerals and I never enjoyed doing mortuary duty which is the lot of hospital chaplains.

'I sing a song of the saints of God'

As I come to end of this memoir I'm thinking of a host of saints who have enriched my life. Pastor Jack Nelson was the nearest person to a father that I had every known. Richard Hendy, maths teacher at Kilkenny College and hockey coach taught me what it was to be a schoolteacher and a hockey player. Bishop George Otto Simms impressed on me words that might have been forgotten – 'Do not forget your ministry'. They were prophetic words indeed. I think too of a simple farmer Dick who did not forget my words in the bank spoken in jest – 'lay not up for yourself treasures on earth'. I think too of the Rev Victor Dungan who taught me courage and integrity and Bishop Noel Willoughby who taught me the value and joy of parish visiting. I think too of the late Jim McAleese who sent me a simple post-card: 'How about Castlepollard and Oldcastle?' I remember the beautiful letter from Siobhan's mother. Siobhan had ovarian cancer and it seemed she would never have children. I encouraged her to look to the light and over the years I baptised three of her children. I think too of George who on my first day in Wexford said 'There was a man sent by God and his name was Norman.'

CHAPTER 30

The Rambling Rector

I was attending an art exhibition at the Wexford Festival some years ago when I came across a painting titled 'The Rambling Rector'. The painting was by a Co Wexford artist, and I was disappointed that I did not buy it. This was the first time that I had learnt that there was a rose called 'The Rambling Rector'. Recently on a visit to Devon with the County Wexford Flower and Garden Club I came across two magnificent specimens of the rose. This was the first time that I had actually seen the rose in bloom. In New Zealand in a bookshop I had seen coloured pictures of it in a book on roses.

I had spent a good deal of time looking for 'The Rambling Rector' and finally found it in my own County of Carlow at Altamount Nurseries, the former home of the late Corona North. She left her garden to the state. The gardener there told me that 'The Rambling Rector' had gone out of fashion because most modern gardens are small, and 'The Rector' is too profuse and grows over too wide an area. It is an old rambling rose which produces a fantastic show of vigorous stems with a sweet scented smell. It has open white flowers with a yellow centre, followed by red hips. The prolific growth can quickly cover an old shed or hedgerow. I've always loved roses and when I had my first garden in Dublin I propagated roses from slips. My interest in roses is being rekindled as I now have more time to do my own thing. Roses can be compared with human beings, for we have to be pruned at times to bring better life and vigour. It is interesting that the Rambling Rector has a vigour and vitality that makes it climb and explore. The rose also needs constant food, and needs to be protected from marauding termites and diseases. The deadwood also needs to be regularly cut away and burnt. When the blooms have gone over, they need to be pruned to make way for new life. In human terms we are not as efficient with people as with roses. People can be like deadwood on committees. They make no contribution, and sit there year after year like the formless bud that never opens. The sap has long since disappeared. If these people were roses they would have long since being dealt with.

'O no man knows through what wild century rolls back the rose'
Managing directors, and bishops are often faced with deadwood, the dead heads that have gone over. They need to be removed or retired to allow others to bear fruit. There are the roses that remain a tight mass, become ugly and never bloom. In a way some clergy have given up for some reason or another. They rarely seek help. The sap has gone out of life, and he or she has lost touch with the tap root. Move the rose, move the rudderless rector to another rectory, which never solves the problem. The gardener has the freedom to dig up the spent rose, but a rector has the right to sit tight. Parsons' freehold gives him or her the freedom to stay put, save for heresy or 'grievous sin'. Some clergy have had to be forcibly removed legally. One cleric who lived in an idyllic rectory refused to move out and anyone who came up the drive would be removed by a pointed shotgun. He had to be brought through the courts, so that the church body could gain possession of the property.

My heart goes out to those priests who are stuck in a rut, and nothing blooms in a rut. A sign in the Australian outback says that if you take this rut it goes on for forty miles, this rut can be a person's fate for forty years.

One clerical colleague took a heavy does of valium before facing a church meeting. He died too young of a broken heart, and he had started out as the most vigorous of climbers. He seemed to die when he lost his sense of humour. The bishop moved him to another parish, but it was like moving from the frying pan into the fire. He was never helped by the institution he served, or maybe he did not want to be helped.

I have always treasured a profuse white rambling rose which grew over a bridge of a small river that runs through Castlecomer in Co Kilkenny. I brought a cutting to Dublin where it grew and grew. From Dublin I brought a cutting to Co Wexford where it quickly covered one side of a courtyard. From

Wexford the rambler travelled to Co Westmeath where it also thrived. Back again to a rectory in Wexford and hopefully its last move will be to my retirement home. Wherever it was planted it spread and brought new life.

When I was in hospital in Belfast my mother brought me the most beautiful red roses from my native Carlow. My tears moistened them for days. It was one of the most beautiful experiences with my mother and she was saying something profound. It was the most intimate time that I had spent with my mother. There is something special about red roses. Older roses too seem to have a more profuse fragrance than the younger varieties.

Thomas Moore's 'The Last Rose of Summer' reminds me of the time when I sang the song at the Feis Ceoil in Dublin. Spring, the ascending sap, Summer the gaiety of colour, Autumn the last blooms and Winter the last disappearing rose. Our human lives fall into the pattern of nature's seasons. 'Grow old along with me, the best is yet to be.'

Recently I was at a Maori festival day in New Zealand and there is a special covered tent for the elderly with refreshments on tap. The Maoris honour old age. The attendant, honouring my age, invited me to sit in the pa (dwelling) especially reserved for the elderly. I have come of age! It reminded me of another occasion in North Carolina when a young boy said to my American friend Joe and myself 'Hello old timers!' I've suddenly realised that Spring, Summer and Autumn have passed and that I've reached the Winter of content. 'The best is yet to be'.